BISON
BOOKS

THE INDIANS OF
SOUTHERN CALIFORNIA
IN 1852

The B. D. Wilson Report
and a Selection of Contemporary Comment

Edited by John Walton Caughey

Introduction to the Bison Books Edition
by Albert L. Hurtado

University of Nebraska Press
Lincoln and London

⊛ The paper in this book meets the minimum requirements of
American National Standard for Information Sciences—Permanence
of Paper for Printed Library Materials, ANSI Z39.48-1984.

First Bison Books printing: 1995
Most recent printing indicated by the last digit below:
10 9   8   7   6   5   4   3   2   1

Library of Congress Cataloging-in-Publication Data
Wilson, Benjamin Davis, 1811–1878.
The Indians of southern California in 1852: the B. D. Wilson report
and a selection of contemporary comment / edited by John Walton
Caughey; introduction to the Bison Books ed. by Albert L. Hurtado.
—Bison Books ed.
p. cm.
Originally published: San Marino, Calif.: Huntington Library, 1952.
The report, prepared in 1852, was originally published serially in the
Los Angeles star, July 18–Sept. 19, 1868.
Includes bibliographical references.
ISBN 0-8032-9776-9 (pbk.: alk. paper)
1. Indians of North America—California. 2. Indians of North
America—Government relations—1789–1869. 3. Indian reserva-
tions—California. I. Caughey, John Walton, 1902–   . II. Title.
E78.C15W55   1996
323.1′970794′09034—dc20
95-23292   CIP

Reprinted from the original 1952 edition by the Henry E. Huntington Library and Art Gallery, San Marino, California.

Grateful acknowledgment is made to Ella Jane Bailey of the University Library at the University of Nebraska at Omaha for providing a
copy of the original for reproduction.

TO LO

CONTENTS

INTRODUCTION TO THE BISON BOOKS EDITION
Albert L. Hurtado

John Walton Caughey edited B. D. Wilson's report on southern California Indians under the most difficult conditions of his professional career. In August of 1950 the Board of Regents had fired him from the UCLA faculty because he refused to sign an oath declaring that he was not a member of the Communist Party. Caughey was not a communist, but he was a staunch civil libertarian who argued that since it was then legal to belong to the Communist Party, the Board of Regents was imposing an unconstitutional political test on university employees. More broadly, Caughey and other faculty believed that the loyalty oath was a threat to academic freedom. Consequently, he and thirty others refused to sign the oath and the regents summarily dismissed them.[1]

In the age of McCarthyism, Caughey paid a high price for his principles. Every major newspaper in California, except the *San Francisco Chronicle,* characterized Caughey and his colleagues as communist dupes and worse. Representatives of the far right were even less complimentary. Bereft of his university salary, Caughey and his family lived first on contributions from those who sympathized with his cause, then on the research stipends from Rockefeller Foundation and American Council of Learned Societies grants. After the grants ran out, Caughey had no income.[2]

Caughey and other fired faculty challenged the acts of the Board of Regents in court, but this was a slow process. In the meantime, he published essays that explained his principles to academe and the general public.[3] In April 1951, the California Third District Court of Appeal ruled that the oath was unconstitutional and threatened academic freedom, thus vindicating Caughey's position. The Board of Regents, however, was not satisfied and appealed to the State Supreme Court. The process took one and a half years more, during which time the regents did not restore the positions of Caughey or his fellow complainants. Finally, late in 1952, the Supreme Court ruled that the oath was unconstitutional, though on much narrower grounds than had the Court of Appeal. Finally, the cashiered professors were permitted to return to their university assignments, but the experience had strongly reinforced Caughey's commitment to civil rights and civil liberties. For the remainder of his career, he and his wife, LaRee Caughey, would write spirited essays and books on academic freedom, civil liberties, and school desegregation.

Caughey learned about liberty, principles, and courage in the American West. He was born in Wichita, Kansas, in 1902, the son of a Presbyterian minister. His family moved several times before settling in Lincoln, Nebraska. A son of the Great Plains, young Caughey matriculated in the University of Texas in 1919. There he majored in English, but he also found time to take history, including some lackluster European courses from a young instructor named Walter Prescott Webb. After graduating, Caughey briefly kept books and then taught for two years at the Schreiner Institute in Kerrville, Texas. Finally, the young bachelor decided to obtain a doctorate and become a professor of history.[4]

Life in Texas had fired Caughey's interest in the history of the West and the American frontier. He had become especially interested in the work of Herbert E. Bolton, formerly on the University of Texas faculty, and now a leading historian at the University of California. Bolton founded the borderlands school of American history—the study of those Spanish possessions that are now part of the United States. His writings augmented the ideas of Frederick Jackson Turner, whose ideas about the American frontier inspired generations of historians—Bolton and Caughey among them. But Turner's vision was essentially Anglocentric as he saw the frontier expand from east to west, influencing the development of American democracy and institutions along the way. Bolton, who studied with Turner at the University of Wisconsin, examined the Spanish frontier and its institutions as they moved out of Mexico. Bolton was a prodigious worker who published many books and articles. Perhaps as important, more than one hundred students finished the Ph.D. under his instruction. Thus, Caughey joined an impressive group of doctoral students who worked with Bolton at Berkeley.[5]

The young doctoral student settled into his dissertation topic, "Louisiana under Spain, 1763–1783," which he completed in 1928. Like all newly minted doctors of philosophy, he then faced the daunting prospect of finding suitable employment. Caughey was fortunate to have studied with Bolton, for his students were in demand and the Berkeley professor worked hard to place them. Even before Caughey finished the degree, Bolton was recommending him to prospective employers.[6] He described Caughey as "brilliant and promising," and a student of "unusual brilliancy," high praise even from Bolton, who was known for hyperbole.[7] Bolton secured a Native Sons of the Golden West Traveling Fellowship for Caughey, which sent him to Spain during the 1928–1929 academic year to gather materials for Bolton's work on Juan Bautista de Anza. While he was in Spain, Caughey completed two articles and asked Bolton to circulate them to journals for him.[8]

In the fall of 1929 Caughey's talent and Bolton's marketing landed a job at San Bernardino Junior College, but he was unhappy there because he had to teach sociology and political science as well as history. Finding that he was unable to pursue his research interests with the heavy teaching load at San Bernardino, Caughey was ready to move to an institution where he could pursue his scholarship. In the next year there was an opening at UCLA, Bolton recommended Caughey, and the university hired him.[9] "What more could you wish," Bolton now asked Caughey, "unless it might be a nice fat salary? I trust that your position will prove to be a permanent one."[10]

Indeed, for twenty years and more Professor Caughey seemed to be a permanent fixture at the "southern branch," as UCLA was then called. He published widely on borderlands topics and eventually concentrated on California history. Caughey was an extremely productive scholar. By 1950 he had published eleven books and forty-nine articles and pamphlets. In 1947 he became the managing editor for the *Pacific Historical Review,* a position that he held until 1968. At the time of the California gold rush centennial, Caughey was acknowledged as a leading scholar of that disorderly era of the state's history.[11]

When Caughey was fired in 1950, he turned his attention to various research projects, including Benjamin D. Wilson's report on southern California Indians. Considering Caughey's long-standing concern with race relations and other matters of justice, it is not surprising that he became interested in Wilson's proposal. The Wilson report dealt with fundamental questions of race, justice, and public policy in the formative years of the state's history.

But the Wilson report did not present a perfect solution for the troubles of the 1850s. In arguing for setting aside a large chunk of Southern California for Indian reservations, Wilson and his silent coauthor, Judge Benjamin Hayes, offered the Franciscan missions as a model for California Indian policy—at least in southern California. Hayes was a Roman Catholic, so it is not surprising that he would find much to praise in the mission system. However, Hayes and Wilson seemed to be unaware of the severe negative impacts that the missions had on native populations, and Caughey did not explain them in his introduction. During the mission era it is now widely accepted that the California Indian population declined from about three hundred thousand to perhaps one hundred seventy-five thousand, mostly due to diseases to which Indians had little resistance. Not well understood in the 1850s, this deadly process had been described and analyzed by the time Caughey wrote his introduction.[12] Caughey seems to accept Wilson and Hayes's argument that, whatever the defects of the missions may have been, they were far more humane and beneficial to the Indians than U.S. Indian policy in the mid-nineteenth century. In the 1950s this was the conventional view that Bolton had established decades earlier.[13] Besides, *some* consistent and rational system had to be adopted, so why not rely on a seemingly successful model from California history? Thus, Wilson and Hayes advocated a reservation system, with a system of missionlike management and compulsory Indian labor as key features.

The recommendations of the Wilson report were never fully carried out because the U.S. Senate refused to ratify treaties that would have reserved lands for Indians. Subsequently, the federal government established temporary Indian reservations that were supposed to be self-sufficient farming establishments operated with compulsory Indian labor—much as Wilson and Hayes had suggested. Three of the reserves (Tejon, Fresno River, and Kings River) were in the region embraced by the report. The temporary reservations were a failure, however, and in the 1860s most of them were abandoned, including Tejon, Fresno River, and Kings River.[14]

It is unlikely that the reservation system that Hayes and Wilson proposed could have succeeded even if it had been implemented as they had envisioned it. The 1850s were a tumultuous decade, Indian rights counted for little among most Californians, and there was constant pressure to drive Indians away and confiscate even the temporary reservations. In the 1850s, the Indian population fell from about one hundred fifty thousand to approximately thirty thousand. In light of all this, it is difficult to view the proposals in the report as a path to Indian salvation that was not taken. Nevertheless, the report remains an important historical document because it describes southern California Indian conditions in the 1850s. It also provides a sense of the limits of what was politically possible at that time; the ideas of Wilson and Hayes crossed that boundary. Even though the authors regarded themselves as benefactors of the Indians, they clearly believed that whites should govern their behavior with a stern, parental hand. It was possible to govern California Indians in this way partly because of their experience in the missions, and partly because the authors believed that these Indians were comparatively docile. Thus, the Indians were prepared to "advance" toward civilization, as Wilson and Hayes understood it. Indian choices and desires were of no particular importance in this matter, except insofar as they seemed to be predisposed to the plan that the southern Californians proposed.

No plan devised by nineteenth-century Anglo-Americans would be entirely satisfying to late-twentieth-century critics. However, it is fair to suggest that Caughey was impressed with the emphasis that the report gave to Indian education. Whatever shortcomings the report may have had, at least it represented an attempt to give Indians the tools with which to live in the now dominant society. Without an adequate education, Caughey believed, minority groups had little chance to compete for jobs, or even to believe in themselves. In that sense, the Wilson report was consonant with Caughey's thinking.

In another way, however, the report was diametrically opposed to Caughey's ideas about education. The proposed schools that the report advocated were presumably segregated because they were located on reservations. Nothing could have been farther from Caughey's philosophy. In the years that followed 1952, Caughey paid increasing attention to the civil rights movement, especially to the problem of de facto school segregation in Los Angeles. Segregation was part of the larger historical fabric of Los Angeles race relations, Caughey argued, which went back to the 1850s when Indian workers were auctioned off in the town plaza.[15] White Angelenos might want to believe that racial discrimination was not an important part of their city's society, but those who looked at the past knew better—and Caughey looked at the past with a cold and penetrating eye that hard experience had washed clean of romantic notions.

Editing the Wilson report did not signal a turning point in Caughey's career, but marked a spot on the consistent trajectory of his professional and civic life. For Caughey there was no clear demarcation between historical scholarship and citizenship. Rather, it became his obligation to apply history to the great task of establishing a just society. Justice, as Caughey knew, often is slow in coming. He was waiting for justice in his case when he wrote the following pages. He also knew that California Indians had waited more than a century for justice—a sobering reminder that justice delayed could result in justice being denied. In Caughey's case at least, justice eventually came. While he waited and after he prevailed, John Walton Caughey went about the business of being an historian and a citizen with high purpose and personal courage.

NOTES

1. John Walton Caughey, *The American West: Frontier and Region,* ed.
Norris Hundley Jr. and John A. Schutz (Los Angeles: The Ward Ritchie
Press, 1969), xvi.

2. Ibid., xviii.

3. See John Walton Caughey, "A Statement of Principles," *Frontier* 1
(15 August 1940): 7–8; Caughey, *A Plea to the Regents of the University of
California* (Los Angeles: privately printed, 1950), a four-page pam-
phlet; Caughey, "A University in Jeopardy," *Harper's Magazine* (November 1950): 68–75; Caughey, "Trustees of Academic Freedom," *Bulletin
of the American Association of University Professors* 37 (1951): 427–41;
Caughey, "Academic Freedom: Bulwark of Democracy," *Bulletin of the
Bureau of School Science* 26 (March 1952): 27–37; Caughey, "The Practical Defense of Academic Freedom," *Bulletin of the American Association
of University Professors* 38 (1952): 244–60.

4. Caughey, *American West,* viii–xi.

5. Caughey reminisced about Berkeley and Bolton in "Herbert Eu-
gene Bolton," in Wilbur R. Jacobs, John W. Caughey, and Joe B. Frantz,
Turner, Bolton, and Webb: Three Historians of the American Frontier (Se-
attle: University of Washington Press, 1965), 41–73. On Bolton, see
John Francis Bannon, *Herbert Eugene Bolton: The Historian and the Man*
(Tucson: University of Arizona Press, 1978).

6. Bolton to Judge G. P. Whittington, 28 February 1928, Herbert Eugene Bolton Papers, Part II, Outgoing Correspondence, Bancroft Library,
University of California, Berkeley (hereafter cited as Bolton Papers, Out).

7. Bolton to Thomas [A.] Bailey, 2 April 1929, Bolton Papers, Out;
Bolton to France Scholes, 2 April 1929, Bolton Papers, Out.

8. Bolton to John F. Davis, 12 April 1929, Bolton Papers, Out. Bolton
did not identify the articles that Caughey had sent him, but likely
candidates are "The Panis Mission to Pensacola, 1778," *Hispanic American Historical Review* 10 (1930): 480–89; "Willing's Expedition down
the Mississippi, 1778," *Louisiana Historical Quarterly* 15 (1932): 5–36;
or "Bernardo de Gálvez and the English Smugglers on the Mississippi,
1777," *Hispanic American Historical Review* 12 (1932): 46–58.

9. Bolton to Joseph Lockey, 8 July 1930, Bolton Papers, Out. See
also Caughey, *American West,* x.

10. Bolton to John Walton Caughey, 17 November 1930, Bolton
Papers, Out.

11. Caughey, *American West,* xiii; for a bibliography of Caughey's
work, complete as of 1969, see 271–77.

12. Sherburne Cook published seminal essays on this subject in the 1940s, reprinted in Cook, *The Conflict between the California Indian and White Civilization* (Berkeley: University of California Press, 1976).

13. Albert L. Hurtado, "Herbert E. Bolton, Racism, and American History," *Pacific Historical Review* 62 (May 1993): 127–42.

14. Albert L. Hurtado, *Indian Survival on the California Frontier* (New Haven: Yale University Press, 1988), 125–48.

15. John Caughey and LaRee Caughey, *School Segregation on Our Doorstep: The Los Angeles Story* (Los Angeles: Quail Books, 1966), 1. See also John Caughey with LaRee Caughey, *To Kill a Child's Spirit: The Tragedy of School Segregation in Los Angeles* (Itasca IL: F. E. Peacock Publishers, 1973).

INTRODUCTION

ON OCTOBER 16, 1852, the editors of the Los Angeles *Star* hailed the appointment of a fellow townsman to federal office. "The universal expression of satisfaction...," they said, "is the surest evidence that the appointment is a good and proper one," and they went on to predict that it would assure "permanent peace with all those tribes which have, in times past, been so troublesome to the country."

The office filled was of modest rank: sub-agent for Indian affairs in southern California. The man appointed—Benjamin Davis Wilson—had already stamped himself as a prominent figure in the community.

A native of Tennessee and eight years a trapper and trader in New Mexico, Wilson had come to California in 1841 with the Workman-Rowland party, the first group of settlers from the United States to enter by the southern route. Already familiar with Spanish American customs, he quickly identified himself with the Californians, to whom he soon was "Don Benito." He married Doña Ramona Yorba, acquired land, and turned ranchero. He earned fame as a bear hunter, incidentally affixing the place name Big Bear Lake, and he also showed a special flair for dealing with the Indians.

In 1845 at Cahuenga, when the adherents of Micheltorena and Alvarado lined up to battle for the governorship, Don Benito helped avert bloodshed. After being taken prisoner at the battle of El Chino in 1846, he served again as mediator in the resolution of the rebellion of the southern Californians against their American conquerors. In the stirring events of '48, '49, and '50, he and his fellow southern Californians were essentially by-standers. They were little disturbed by the persistence of military government, only moderately aroused by the gold rush, and less inclined than those in the north to exult over statehood. Gold did boom the market for beef and mutton. Wilson engaged in cattle and sheep drives north, his ranch operations became more profitable, and so did his merchant business in Los Angeles.

Thus in 1852, at forty-one, besides being a former mayor of Los Angeles and the county clerk, he was one of the older American residents and a leading merchant and landowner. He can hardly have regarded the post of sub-agent for Indian affairs as a great plum. In reporting his appointment, therefore, the *Star* was probably correct in identifying his reason for accepting the office as "a desire to secure peace and justice to the Indians" and "to render to the government of the United States whatsoever service may be in his power."

On his qualifications for the job there is direct testimony in the form of a thumbnail sketch written a few months later by a close acquaintance, Judge Benjamin Hayes:

"Mr. Wilson," he wrote, "is an old mountaineer, and a gentleman in every sense of the word. He is wealthy and independent—and so does not need this office. His wealth has come to him in a measure suddenly, by the rise of property; after many 'hard knocks' in the Rocky Mountains and here, before, during and since the war. He has been in some little campaigns formerly against portions of these Indians, and knows them, and they know him well. Before his appointment, their Chiefs visiting the City, habitually came to see and talk with him about their business, as much as if he were their

Agent. Notoriously he is a favorite with them—no stranger. His good sense, kindness of heart, knowledge of mountain life, familiarity with all the tribes, and reputation for integrity of purpose are difficult to combine in any one else that may be recommended from this quarter."[1]

In the course of the following decades Don Benito went on to higher honors and more substantial rewards. He served on the San Gabriel school board and in the state senate. He was stockholder and director in southern California's earliest oil, telegraph, and railroad companies and participated in several water development projects. He was a leading orchardist, vineyardist, and vintner. Having progressed from stock raising to horticulture, he took up real estate subdividing and promotion. Still later his fame was enhanced by the phenomenal development of the lands he once owned at Riverside, San Marino, Pasadena, and Westwood, by the astronomical observatory and the television transmitters on Mt. Wilson, and by the distinguished careers of a number of his descendants, notably General George S. Patton.

Definitive history probably will record the agricultural and business chapters as the most significant in his life work. Nevertheless, in 1877, when historian Hubert Howe Bancroft asked for a biographical statement, Wilson's one request was that he be remembered as a friend of the Indians and credited with urging their settlement on reservations.[2] The plan alluded to is set forth in detail in the report that comprises the body of this volume.

[1] Benjamin Hayes to Senator David R. Atchison, January 14, 1853, draft, Hayes Scrapbooks, Bancroft Library, XXXIX, 121 (reproduced below, pp. 82-86).
[2] Hubert Howe Bancroft, *History of California* (7 vols., San Francisco, 1884-1890), V, 777.

THE LOCALE

The locale of this report—southern California from the Colorado to the Pacific and from the Mexican border to the southern San Joaquin Valley—is a large area in which all of New England could be contained. Today it has a great variety of proven resources and a population of five or six millions. As of 1852 it was an undeveloped and all but empty land. Its *gente de razón*, in free translation its "civilized inhabitants," numbered hardly more than five or six thousand, or one tenth of one per cent of today's census.

Politically this territory had been organized, somewhat reluctantly, as the southern counties of the newly erected state. The men of San Francisco and the diggings condescendingly referred to it as the Cow Counties. And they were right, not merely in terms of the ranchos with their thousands of head of cattle, which were the sinew of the region, but also in terms of the habits and interests of the people, the general backwardness of the economy, and the primitive character of society. True enough, the talisman of gold had recently shifted the emphasis from hides to beef and was encouraging actual cultivation of the soil. According to the state census of 1852, Los Angeles County, with less than a fiftieth of the state's population, had a quarter of the cattle, a fifth of the horses, and a twentieth of the cultivated acreage.

In a land so thoroughly agricultural, it is something of a paradox to find most of the people living in town. Of course, the Spanish American frontier had stressed agricultural villages rather than single-family farms. Irrigation likewise meant intensive cultivation of compact tracts rather than the tilling of widely scattered fields. And cattle raising on the open range, whatever its other merits, did not call for a large labor force constantly spread out over the entire grazing area. Moreover, especially in the case of the more inland ranchos, the exposure to Indian raids from the wilder hinterland encouraged a clustering in the towns, and the general remoteness of the region probably had similar effect. For these reasons and perhaps others the towns had special importance.

Near each of the old mission sites there was at least a nucleus of settlement, the most flourishing being San Diego, where the colonization of California had started in 1769, and Santa Barbara, which dated from 1786. As of 1852, however, the more populous centers were at San Bernardino, where five hundred Latter-day Saints had recently arrived to establish a Mormon outpost, and in the metropolis of the south, with perhaps two thousand souls assembled in the City of the Angels.

Consisting mainly of single-story adobe buildings straggling out from a central plaza, Los Angeles had the innocent appearance of a little Spanish town. The speech and dress of most of its people and a good fraction of the social practices also reflected the Spanish and Mexican background. On a smaller scale it presented many of the characteristics which American visitors found so striking in Santa Fe.

By 1852, however, Los Angeles' Spanish appearance was somewhat deceiving, for many elements of the local scene had the unmistakable flavor of the United States, or, more distinctively, of the American West. At times the town was boisterous with freighters and muleskinners from the Salt Lake line. Its status as a cow town gave it some of the toughness soon to be associated with Abilene and Dodge City. Its population was also swelled with adventurers from the gold fields and with hard characters who had fled from the vigilantes of San Francisco.

These newcomers, along with the handful of Anglo-Americans of longer residence, of whom Wilson is an excellent example, were the culture-bearers of the new civilization. They brought new blood, a new language, new laws, a new basis for land ownership, new social practices, and a new perspective on race relationships. Under their tutelage southern California was in process of transition from Spanish to American ways. More precisely, an aggressive American frontier was being superimposed on an older Spanish frontier that had not had time to run its full course.

Published reminiscences, contemporary letters such as those in the Stearns and Wilson papers at the Huntington Library, and the broken files of the newspapers of the day give a vivid picture of the times. Politically, the southern Californians were full of complaints. They did not like the federal act which unsettled practically all land titles and subjected the claimants to long and expensive litigation. They felt that the national government should do more than it had in the assignment of troops to the region and to improve transportation and mail service. Displeased with statehood because of the dominance of the north and the heavy burden of real estate taxes, they clamored for state division and the erection of a territorial government in the south. Economically the region was thoroughly subservient to San Francisco. The northern part of the state was the sole market for the produce of southern ranchos, farms, and gardens, and the coastal steamers and sailing schooners from San Francisco brought in return the merchandise for local consumers. They also brought whatever news there was of the outside world.

Some of the descriptive items found in these various sources have no very profound significance—for example, the comment on the superabundance of dogs in Los Angeles, a newspaperman's difficulties in collecting accounts, or a passing craze for bear cubs as pets. Others prick out the intercultural factor. In the recreational field, for example, *bailes* (Spanish dances) were the most popular events. One at Abel Stearns' home, on Washington's Birthday in 1853, led to a riot when uninvited guests tried to join in. Six weeks later, at the conclusion of Lent, the *Star* reported "a grand cock-fight...on the Plaza, opposite the Church, made up between Don Pio Pico and Mr. John Powers." Then came a race "between Moore and Brady's horse, John Smith, and Mr. J. Powers' mare, Sarah Jane, for $2,100 a side, which the horse won by about a length. This was decidedly the prettiest race we have seen in the city. After the race a game of 'shinty' was played between a party of twelve Americans against twelve Californians, on the result of which about $1500 was bet. That was fine sport. The men on each side were strong, athletic, nimble fellows, selected expressly for their supposed proficiency in the game, and at the commencement bets were about even...."

On May 14, 1853, the *Star* reported further on the recreational activities of the community, this time running true to the form of the American frontier. "The 'Bar'," it reported, "was out in full force last evening, in commemoration of some event or events to our reporter unknown, and perambulated the streets until a late hour, very kindly preventing the citizens from over indulging themselves in a sort of imaginary luxury called sleep, and setting a fine example to Indians and rowdies generally, which we have no doubt they will be quick enough to imitate. The whole affair ended in a row, in which the only sufferer was our city Marshall, who it is said sustained a dental attack upon the most prominent and one of the most useful and ornamental portions of his face. His adversary, whoever he was, displayed a most anti-epicurean taste."

Equally routine as an American frontier item was the *Star*'s scornful comment, December 22, 1855, on a new city ordinance prohibiting the discharge of pistols within the city limits. The council, it said, might as well have outlawed smoking. Who has not fired a pistol in the streets, it asked, and who has been fined for doing it?

With such a volatile and unrestrained population, with knives and guns so plentiful, and with the restraining arm of government imperfectly developed, crimes of violence were all too common. Reminiscence has magnified them to "a murder a day," or "a dead man for breakfast every morning," or to three or four violent deaths per diem, at which rate the Los Angeles population would hardly have lasted the year. Scanning the papers, and bearing in mind that they were weeklies, one does get the impression that almost every issue had a homicide to report. The casual treatment of some of these stories suggests that they had almost ceased to be news. On May 14, 1853, for example, there was a laconic note on an inquest on the body of an Indian found near the zanja with his throat cut. The verdict is described as "the customary one," perhaps in the phraseology elsewhere recorded, "Death by an unknown hand or by a visitation from God."

There were spectacular crimes too. In the summer of 1852 two Americans disappeared after being last seen in the company of a certain Doroteo Savaleta, who had subsequently displayed $500 in American gold. "Travelers are not safe," the *Star* editorialized on July 24, "until a gang of desperadoes, of which Savaleta is but one, is exterminated." "We are indebted," the story continued, "for the above particulars to B. D. Wilson, Esq., who has been actively engaged in endeavoring to ascertain the fate of the two Americans alluded to."

A week later, in a three-column story, the *Star* told of the arrest at Santa Barbara of Savaleta and Jesús Rivas, their return to Los Angeles, trial by a people's court, and prompt execution atop Fort Moore Hill. Although a few months earlier the *Star* had been critical of vigilante justice, it now took lynch law as a matter of course.

The following November popular resentment mounted still higher over the assassination of the debonair and popular Joshua H. Bean. A volunteer tribunal swung into action, laid hold of a number of suspects, put them through a grilling, extracted from one a confession of other crimes, and heard explicit charges that Cipriano Sandoval, San Gabriel shoemaker, was the man who had killed Bean. By the hour set for the executions, three o'clock of a Sunday afternoon, the committee had a third candidate, caught that morning in the act of stabbing a companion. The three were hanged. Five years later, the real murderer of Bean made a death-bed confession which established Sandoval's innocence. A regular court, of course, might have made the same error, but the impetuosity of lynch law puts it in special hazard of mistaking identity or acting upon insufficient evidence.

These are but two of many vigilante executions at Los Angeles in the fifties. Quick and severe though punishment had become, it did not seem to prevent crime. In 1854 the San Francisco *Herald* reported receipt of a letter from an Angeleño who said it was unsafe to go out after dark. The *Herald* had no better cure to suggest than vigilante action such as San Francisco had employed in '51—and would need again in '56 —and Los Angeles already had that device going full blast.

A more perspicacious analysis had been offered by the San Francisco *Alta California* on July 23, 1853. "Los Angeles County," it observed, "affording as it does temptation, as well as facilities to murderers and robbers, has long been to Northern California what Texas was formerly to the States—a rendezvous for villains." The phrase "Gone to Los Angeles" never achieved the full flavor, even locally, that had attached to "Gone to Texas," but by all accounts the analogy drawn by the *Alta* was valid.

One other fact is underlined in the primary descriptions of southern California in the early fifties, namely, the size and significance of the Indian element. In this part of the state they were well in the majority and, though far from being the ruling class, they were of substantial importance.

INDIAN BACKGROUNDS

Earliest reports of the southern California Indians depict an affable, hospitable people, most primitive in skills and possessions, but subsisting comfortably on what the land and the sea offered. To some casual observers the ultra-simplicity looked like miserable poverty. At the other extreme is some more recent anthropological opinion that it was a good life with plenty of food, much leisure, and a great deal of fun.

Taken in hand by the Franciscan missionaries late in the eighteenth century, the Indians near the coast began the arduous process of learning the ways of the white man and adjusting to them. The process was gradual and slow. It included instruction in the religion and language of Spain. It called for changes in dress and deportment. It meant getting used to a different sort of dwelling and to new rules of social relations. It involved learning how to work at various tasks which the Spaniards regarded as useful: at gardening and stock tending, at the so-called mission industries such as soap making and tile making, at the simpler building trades, and in other forms of skilled or semi-skilled labor. Although not the most apt pupils that the New World had offered, these Indians traveled a long distance along the mission road. They picked up many elements of Spanish civilization and got to be culturally far removed from the untutored tribesmen of the mountain and desert interior.

In the thirties, after the older missions had run about sixty years and the later ones long enough to have primarily a mission-born clientele, secularization was suddenly ordered. True, the aim of the mission program had been to train the Indians to the point where they could be released from mission discipline and take their place as full-fledged subjects of the Spanish monarch. In the thirties no one seriously contended that the Californians had come so far. But there were men who coveted the mission lands and herds, and it was possible to argue that the mission system was an anachronism in the Mexican republic. Abruptly the Indians were turned loose. A few may have bettered themselves at once. A larger number went off to the interior and went native or, in more elaborate expression, reverted to barbarism. Most of the former mission Indians tarried in the mission area, which after all was their ancestral home. Ill prepared to manage their own affairs, they took whatever jobs they could get, and many of them lapsed into dissipation and debauchery.

In mission days the Indians had become accustomed to week-end rations of *aguardiente*. In their independent status the tendency was to place still more emphasis on this custom and some of them carried it to excess. Drunkenness and fighting, sometimes with fatal result, came to be regular Saturday night behavior in Los Angeles' Nigger Alley, giving the peace officers the routine task of locking up sundry drunks, most of whom were Indians. In court on Monday morning fines would be assessed, and if, as frequently was the case, the Indians could not pay they would be bound out to an employer to work it off.

This Los Angeles "slave mart" came in for some criticism in its day and for more bitter condemnation by later writers. One may extenuate by pointing out that the benevolent Walter Colton, American alcalde at Monterey, had used the same method, and that week by week the Indian auction involved only a small fraction of the total labor force. Nevertheless, it does betray a callousness about human rights, and of course the real flaw was in encouraging the conditions which produced carousing and drunkenness.

The southern Californians of the fifties were much more concerned about another aspect of the Indian problem, the habit of bands from the Mojave Desert and beyond to cross the mountains and raid the ranchos. These Indians killed a few head of cattle, but primarily they were after horses, which were easier to drive away and sweeter to the taste. Raids of this type had occurred in the Mexican period, and on two such occasions Wilson had led pursuits across the mountains and out upon the desert.

After the American conquest the marauders became bolder. In May, 1849, there was a raid on Rancho Azusa. In June another band swept almost to Los Angeles, picking off a drove of horses with which it headed back toward Cajon Pass. There Abel Stearns and a volunteer crew overtook the raiders and recovered the horses, killing ten of the Indians and losing two of their own number.

In January, 1850, Deputy Sheriff A. P. Hodges mustered forty-seven well-armed men to track down another horse-stealing band. According to Horace Bell, they rode forth bravely, but stopped to fortify themselves with food and drink at every rancho, and on the third day despaired of overtaking their quarry. But according to Judge Benjamin Hayes, "the state ought to pay the expenses of this volunteer expedition," and he forwarded the tab to a member of the state legislature, which was just starting its first session.

A year later raiders from the desert ran off the entire horse herd from José María Lugo's rancho, some seventy-five head. This time pursuit was more rapid. The thieves were overtaken about 100 miles beyond Cajon Pass, but the pursuers were fifteen against fifty. They found the Indians on the alert and well armed, and after losing one man in the first fusillade they were forced to turn back emptyhanded.

Another danger spot was at Four Creeks in the southern San Joaquin Valley, near present-day Visalia. In 1851 Henry Dalton and a Captain Dorsey from San Jose lost men and horses and cattle as they were trailing beeves to the northern market. The next year a trail herd of 2,000 head of cattle was run off and several vaqueros were killed. Meanwhile, raids on the exposed ranchos continued. Indeed, the editor of the Los Angeles *Star* in 1855, in casting up accounts on losses from San Diego to San Luis Obispo, put the 1849-53 total at not less than $300,000 in horses alone.

Whether or not his figure was actuarially sound, these raids were not merely a nuisance, but a serious threat to the prosperity and security of southern California. Furthermore, there was always the possibility that the condition would get worse. If the Indians nearer the coast—the central figures in Wilson's report—should adopt the hostility of those farther inland, the danger and the damage could be ever so much greater.

In December, 1851, just such an outbreak seemed to be in the making. Led by Antonio Garrá, of the Warner's Ranch district, the Indians of the southern mountain area took up arms, plundered Warner's Ranch, and threatened to kill all the whites in southern California. The Mormons at San Bernardino hurriedly erected a stockade. Los Angeles sent out a

posse under Joshua Bean. But it was Juan Antonio, the Cahuilla chief, who quelled the uprising. He took Garrá into
custody and turned him over to Bean. At San Diego there
was the formality of a trial and Garrá, still obdurate, was executed. This insurrection had, for the whites, a happy ending, but it was a forceful reminder of the precariousness of
life on this Indian frontier.

STATE AND FEDERAL POLICY

Since in American practice Indian affairs have been more the
function of the state than of the local unit, it was natural that
the California state government, when it began to operate, in
the winter of 1849-50, should pay some attention to the problem. To say that the state adopted an Indian policy would exaggerate, but it did set in motion a program that was simple,
direct, and vigorous.

The opinion then current among Californians, most of
whom were not in contact with the southern California Indians of the following report, was that destiny had awarded
California to the Americans to develop, that the aborigines
were no asset to the state, and that wherever they interfered
with progress they should be pushed aside. The state proceeded to implement this opinion by authorizing military
campaigns against Indians alleged to have committed depredations and by accepting the bills for such work as a charge
against the state treasury.

The result was one of the most disgraceful chapters in the
entire history of the state. Armed bands took the field against
the Indians on an almost completely indiscriminate basis. A
whole series of Indian "wars" ensued, though, as Bancroft
sagely observed, there was not a respectable one in the lot.
Instead they featured wholesale butchery and seemed to aim

at complete liquidation of the Indians. The following oratorical outburst, which Horace Bell intended as hyperbole, is in
fact a reasonably accurate statement of the code that then prevailed."We will let those rascally redskins know that they
have no longer to deal with the Spaniard or the Mexican, but
with the invincible race of American backwoodsmen, which
has driven the savage from Plymouth Rock to the Rocky
Mountains, and has headed him off here on the western shore
of the continent, and will drive him back to meet his kindred
fleeing westward, all to be drowned in the great Salt Lake."[3]

The brunt of this attack fell farther north, but there were
southern repercussions. There was, for example, a campaign
against the Yumas late in 1850. Its occasion was the killing of
eleven Colorado River ferrymen, headed by John Glanton.
In Los Angeles Glanton and his associates were regarded as
cutthroats and robbers and there was no enthusiasm about
avenging them. But by recruiting newly arrived emigrants,
Joseph R. Morehead got together 125 men, descended on
the Yumas, and killed a score of them. The expense account,
sometimes cited as the main consequence, ran to $76,588.

Meanwhile, the federal government, normally the main reliance in Indian matters, extended a faltering hand toward
California.The distance was great, and the information about
the region was none too reliable. Expansion to the Pacific had
come suddenly, and the Indian office operated under laws
designed for a much smaller West. In part because appointments were political there was a rapid turnover in the per-
sonnel assigned to California, and relatively few showed aptitude for the work. The outrageous prices of the gold rush
inflation made it difficult to finance the program adequately,
and this circumstance led some of the agents into most un-

[3] Horace Bell, *Reminiscences of a Ranger* (Los Angeles, 1881), 116.

businesslike dealings. Yet the main handicap probably was that there was a basic disagreement between federal intentions and the wishes of the majority of Californians.

As early as April, 1847, General S. W. Kearny, in his capacity as military governor, appointed Indian agents for three districts: north of San Francisco Bay, the Central Valley, and southern California. Since the problem was not acute the agents did little. The next year Mexico ceded the entire area to the United States in a treaty that came to be interpreted, most unfortunately, as an absolute dispossession of the California Indians. In 1849 a State Department emissary, Thomas Butler King, urged attention to the problem. That same year, under the newly created Department of the Interior, a California Indian agent was appointed, a certain John Wilson, no kin of B. D. He was assigned to "Salt Lake City, California," which turned out not to be in the state after all. At the same time, Adam Johnston was named sub-agent for the Sacramento-San Joaquin Valley. His first report, dated January 31, 1850, dealt with the plight of the former mission Indians and their need for an assignment of land. Then he went to the Central Valley and undertook to do something for the Indians there.

Late in 1850, with a $50,000 appropriation as backing, the Indian Office sent three commissioner-agents to California with specific instructions to negotiate treaties assigning specific tracts to the various California tribes.

Reaching California early in 1851, the three commissioners were soon at work negotiating treaties. At first they worked as a team, going with military escort, supplies, and presents to the eastern margin of the San Joaquin Valley, where on March 19 they concluded a treaty with six tribes or bands of "Mountain and Mercede Indians" and on April 19 with another sixteen tribes or bands. Then they decided to split up, Redick McKee moving into the northern part of the state, O. M. Wozencraft continuing in the middle district, and George W. Barbour taking the south. Within a year they had negotiated eighteen treaties embracing 139 tribes or bands, promising annuities of beef, blankets, and other supplies, and in the aggregate setting aside 7,488,000 acres, or about a fourteenth of the total area of the state, as permanent domicile for these Indians. With insignificant exceptions the lands involved had no white occupants or claimants and were regarded by the commissioners as relatively worthless. Most of the tracts were on the floor of the Central Valley, before long to prove fabulously productive.

The work of the commissioners aroused a great clamor. The Department of the Interior was displeased that on a budget of $50,000 they had purchased and contracted to the tune of $716,394.79. Some claims were paid; others were protested. The eighteen treaties were submitted to the Senate. Deluged with protests from California citizens, mindful of the opposition of the California delegation in the Congress, and influenced no doubt by the thought that much of this land might prove to be gold-bearing, the Senate refused all eighteen treaties. Belatedly, in 1944, the United States Court of Claims awarded some five million dollars as compensation to the California Indians for losses suffered through the nonfulfillment of these treaties. The money was later appropriated and impounded for ultimate use in a manner or manners still to be determined.

It was in this setting of confused plans, in the fall of 1852, that Edward F. Beale came to California as the newly appointed superintendent of Indian affairs. A veteran officer in the Navy, companion of Kit Carson in the hazardous exploit of going through the Californian lines to get help for Kearny's dragoons after the battle of San Pascual, and courier with the first California gold delivered to the capital in Washington, Beale was a man of parts. He was more intent on achieving tangible benefits for his Indian wards than any of his predecessors had been. It was he who chose Wilson as sub-agent for southern California, and it was at his request that this report on the Indians of the area was written.

THE REPORT AND ITS RECEPTION

Even the most casual reading of the report discloses a far more polished style than characterizes Wilson's other writings. Since the report survives in the form in which it was printed in 1868 in the Los Angeles *Star*, it is possible of course that the editor at that time regularized the spelling and punctuation and elevated the rhetoric. The differences, however, extend further. The vocabulary is considerably more elaborate and learned than Wilson customarily used, and the periods are often much more oratorical. There also are passages that suggest the legal mind at work and others which would have come more naturally from a devout Roman Catholic. The indications thus are that Wilson had assistance.

An entry under date of January 1, 1853, in Benjamin Hayes' diary makes this much more explicit. "In the afternoon," this entry reads, "finished the map to accompany the report of Indian Agent (Benj. D. Wilson). Mr. Wilson, in this matter, is acting with a spirit of philanthropy most honorable to him. This Report is of date December 26, 1852, prepared by me, at his instance, from information derived from Don Juan Bandini, Hon. J. J. Warner, and Hugo Reid, Esq. One copy for the Superintendent, Lt. E. Beale; with the other, Mr.

Wilson goes to the Legislature, now in session, to obtain their
co-operation in his plans for the Old Mission Indians."[4]

The phrase, "prepared by me," might signify merely that
Hayes was a one-man committee on style, smoothing the
rough places in Wilson's draft. In the context, however, it
seems to mean much more. Its assertion really is that Hayes
actually composed the report and that he thereby qualifies
as Los Angeles' first ghost writer. Several things about him
point up the possibility that he could have done it.

A Missourian, Hayes set out for California as a forty-niner.
He was so long en route that he did not get to Los Angeles
until early 1850. He began practice of law at once and in the
1852 election was chosen first district judge for southern California. He continued on the bench through 1864. Along with
the dispensing of justice he combined many other activities.
He was an inveterate correspondent to the newspapers and
often a contributor of editorials. For the whole period of his
residence in southern California, from 1850 to 1877, he kept
a careful meteorological record. He was also a self-appointed
archivist of local history. By personal observation and by
questioning older residents he gathered information about
the region's past and when manuscript or printed materials
came his way he preserved them. He thus was a treasure trove
for Hubert Howe Bancroft when that collector-historian cast
his net in the southern part of the state. Hayes, in fact, turned
over his collection to Bancroft and became his agent in trans-
cribing the official records of Los Angeles. It was with some
bias then, but not with complete inaccuracy, that Bancroft
said of Hayes that, however creditable his career as a jurist,
he "performed for his country, for the world, for posterity, a

[4] Marjorie Tisdale Wolcott, ed., *Pioneer Notes from the Diaries of Judge
Benjamin Hayes*, 1849-1875 (Los Angeles, 1929), 94.

work beside which sitting upon a judicial bench and deciding cases was no more than catching flies."[5]

As a close personal friend of Wilson's, as a lawyer and a Roman Catholic, by reason of his genuine concern for the Indians, by reason of his penchant for local history and anti-quarianism, and particularly by reason of his well known propensity for writing, Hayes was the logical person for the desk work involved in formulating this long and elaborate report.

If he did ghost write it, an added fillip is given Hayes' enthusiastic endorsement of the document, a fortnight later, in a letter to his old friend, David R. Atchison, United States Senator from Missouri. "Let me beg you," he wrote, "to notice the Report of the Indian agent for this District, Benjamin D. Wilson, Esq. I am acquainted, of my own knowledge, with nearly all the facts stated by him.... I have given no little attention to the subject—more I suspect, than any other resident here, unless I except Mr. Wilson."[6]

All of which, however, is not to say that Wilson's name is improperly attached to the report. At the time and ever since, it has been known as his. Hayes' diary makes passing reference to it as Wilson's in the entry for January 5, 1853. Wilson's intimate knowledge of the Indians far transcended Hayes'. He was vitally concerned about their welfare and thoroughly believed in the solution proposed in the report. It may well have been his in conception, and he certainly made it his in execution. Therefore, whether Hayes was editorial consultant or ghost writer, there is an abiding justification for referring to the document as the Wilson report.

In appraising the Indian problem of southern California, the report saw two factors involved. One was the matter of

[5] Hubert Howe Bancroft, *Literary Industries* (San Francisco, 1890), 479.
[6] Hayes to Atchison, January 14, 1853, loc. cit.

guarding against raids upon the ranchos and settlements. The other was to rescue the former mission Indians from the deterioration into which they had been plunged and to help them toward self-sufficiency and greater civic usefulness.

Reviewing recent practices, the report noted that there had been heavy dependence on military campaigns which were strictly punitive, and on the handing out of presents, most generously to the Indians who had caused the most trouble. Both devices had been expensive and neither had proved effective. The interests of the peaceable Indians meanwhile had been almost entirely neglected. Opposed to spasmodic military ventures as extravagant and to indiscriminate present-giving as demoralizing, the report looked elsewhere for a solution. The genius of its proposal was that through one device it would tackle the problem of curbing hostilities and the problem of regenerating the former mission Indians.

The device, the reservation system, was not a Wilsonian invention. The famous program of removing the eastern Indians to a permanent Indian territory west of the Mississippi had employed elements of the scheme. The California treaty-makers of 1851 were also working toward concentrating the Indians on assigned tracts. Beale had endorsed this program before coming to California. His plan involved not merely the assembling of the Indians on these reserves, but also their practical instruction in farming, blacksmithing, and other manual arts. This, in fact, was a feature of United States Indian policy dating back to the nation's first years.

What Wilson was in position to add came from his personal knowledge of the Indians of southern California. The report stressed the progress they had made as neophytes at the missions and their nostalgia for those good old days. On this point it probably exaggerated. But there was confidence that life on a constructively programmed reservation could be made attractive and rewarding and that the more practical features of the old mission system could be revived. The missions had been self-supporting, even prosperous. There was no reason why reservations could not do as well. As contrasted to the debits for Indian wars and presents, the funds laid out for reservation development should have the character of investments.

In essence, Wilson's report, besides describing the local Indian scene, amplified the project of establishing reservations and invoked California history of the Spanish period as a justification of the plan. In addition, it could point out that since white settlement was almost entirely confined to the coastal plain and its tributary valleys, the land lay open for the reservation experiment.

Not long after its submission, the report came to the attention of the editors of the Los Angeles *Star*. They noted, on January 15, 1853, that "it suggests a plan for the future government of the Indians, strictly philanthropic, and which, if carried out cannot fail to benefit a people once more than half civilized, but now exhibiting such signs of retrogression and decay as must be deplored by every humane heart."

"The report," the *Star* continued, "contains a vast fund of information, and the publication of it will be an important addition to the cause of science. The views of Mr. Wilson touching the management of the Indians become important at this time, when the whole course of Legislation seems tending toward the extermination of the Indian race. If the government of the United States desires the preservation of the Indians, some system must be adopted similar to that proposed by Mr. Wilson. It could be put into operation here most effectually, for the tribes hereabout have a vivid recollection of the 'good old days' of the Missions, and they desire now, more than ever before, the protection and care of their white neighbors."

Benjamin Hayes also endorsed the proposal. To Senator Atchison of Missouri he wrote on January 14, 1853, "This Report ought to be printed by Congress and circulated generally in this State and elsewhere. It presents the true plan for managing these Indians. And the boldness with which he asserts the legal right of the Mission Indians to their property, in the face of the *speculators* in Mission titles, some of them otherwise his bosom friends, might immortalize some men, even of greater ability and in a higher station."

THE FIRST RESERVATION

Beale, of course, was already persuaded that the program was advisable. Although the treaties that might have permitted a start had been rejected, he proposed a series of military posts which might be used as Indian refuges—reservations in all but title. The association of military post and Indian reservation was not ideal, but it seemed to be the only way to get approval for the latter. Beale's urging of a $500,000 appropriation fell on deaf ears. Early in 1853, however, he went to Washington and on March 3 had the pleasure of seeing Congress authorize as many as five military reservations in California at which Indians might be assembled, with $250,000 appropriated for the purpose.

Returning overland to California, Beale set to work in the early fall of 1853 to get the pilot reservation established. He and Wilson held several parleys with the Indians of the Tejon Pass region. Not all were persuaded to adopt reservation life, but others were brought from as far away as the Mother Lode region, and by the following February Beale could report 2,500 Indians in the mission-like community over which he presided. They had planted 2,000 acres in wheat, 500 in barley, and 150 in corn, and were at work on ditches to irrigate and enclose their fields. The first crop was reported at 42,000 bushels of wheat and 10,000 of barley. According to Beale's glowing description, the Tejon, or Sebastian, reservation was such a success that other groups of Indians were eager to move in and enjoy the same privileges. He hoped to enlarge the Tejon and to develop other sites.

In the summer of 1854, however, Beale was suddenly removed from office. There were charges that his financial accounts were not in order and insinuations, subsequently disproved, that he had been guilty of peculations. His immediate successor continued the Tejon reservation and established others in northern California. He in turn was charged with misuse of funds, apparently on valid grounds. Other superintendents followed in rapid succession, few of them as much interested in the welfare of the Indians as in turning a profit, and under their control the reservations steadily worsened. Before long it was evident that the fine results that Wilson had envisioned and that Beale found almost within his grasp were not going to be achieved.

As early as 1858 J. Ross Browne was ready to condemn the system out of hand. Commissioned to inspect the Indian work in California, he visited the Mendocino reservation and submitted an adverse report. His findings were also made public in 1861 in an ironic, trenchant, mordant paper for *Harper's Magazine*. He defined the reservation as a place "where a very large amount of money was annually expended in feeding white men and starving Indians" and "where a gratifying scene might be witnessed, at no remote period, of big and little Diggers holding forth from every stump in support of the presiding administration." Referring specifically to California he concluded that in a brief period of six years the Indians had been nearly destroyed by the generosity of government. They were suffering, he said, for "the great cause of civilization, which, in the natural course of things, must exterminate Indians."

Throughout California Indian numbers rapidly declined. In the south, the area they occupied dwindled to a small fraction of the vast estate described by Wilson in 1852. Where they retained occupancy of a small tract, more often than not it was with imperfect title. At the turn of the century, with increasing white pressure for their lands, the southern California tribesmen needed a new champion in Charles F. Lummis and his Sequoyah League to assure them even a modicum of justice.

In general American practice, however, the reservation system caught on. It became the key device for federal administration of Indian affairs.

EXHUMING THE REPORT

After the first flurry of attention from Beale, Hayes, and the editors of the *Star*, Wilson's report fell into the limbo of things forgotten. In 1868 it was rescued temporarily through publication in ten installments in the Los Angeles *Star*, July 18–September 19. A complete run of the *Star* has not been preserved, but the Bancroft Library file includes these particular issues, and Benjamin Hayes' busy scissors also clipped it for his scrapbooks, later consigned to the Bancroft collection. A number of modern researchers have cited the serialized report, but it is a safe supposition that very few persons have read it through since the time of its newspaper appearance.

At the time of that printing, on August 1, 1868, an editorial in the *Star* opined that the document was interesting, not only as it concerned "the aboriginal races of Southern California," but more especially "in a historical point of view, as showing the condition of the country in the early days treated of."

At this much later date other elements of value can be seen. For example, the report sheds much light on the qualities and character of B. D. Wilson. He was one of the more appealing of the American pioneers, significant in his own right, and something of a type in southern California's period of transition from Spanish to American ways. The report is a contribution toward the biography of Wilson that someday will be written, and perhaps toward that of Benjamin Hayes.

In mid-twentieth century, too, a more responsive note can be counted on for the analysis of the region's Indians, their past experiences, their problems, and the proffered solution. The document will be recognized as having value both to those whose interest is in the Indian as an anthropological specimen and to those whose primary concern is in the study of American Indian policy.

Nevertheless, the chief reason for turning to the report today may be, as it was in 1868, its usefulness "in a historical point of view, as showing the condition of the country in the early days treated of."

Here the document is allowed to speak for itself, with only a minimum of editorial annotation. To it is added a group of comments on Indian affairs in southern California in the period of the report. They have been gleaned from the early press and from other fugitive sources. Some relate to Indian behavior in Los Angeles, some to hostilities committed, some to the reservation system, some to Wilson's report. They illustrate further the problems to which his report was addressed and suggest what its effects were and what they might have been.

THE INDIANS OF SOUTHERN
CALIFORNIA IN 1852

THE REPORT

SIR: IN COMPLIANCE with your request, of date 19th ult., I proceed to give you my views upon the policy most proper to be adopted by the General Government towards the Southern Indians of California. Of them I can speak more confidently than of those in other parts of the State. With suitable modifications, the same policy may be found applicable to all.

At present, I must necessarily confine myself to the Indians living on the borders of, or within the district of country embracing the counties of Tulare (in part), Santa Barbara, Los Angeles, and San Diego;[7] and, particularly, to that portion of them who have been for a great many years in more immediate contact with the influences of civilization.

The Indians thus deserving particular notice are the Tulareños, Cahuillas, San Luiseños, and Dieguiños.[8] All of these were attached to the Missions, more or less.

[7] By process of division these counties have multiplied and now comprise Tulare, Kings, Inyo, Kern, Santa Barbara, Ventura, Los Angeles, San Bernardino, Orange, Riverside, San Diego, and Imperial. See Owen C. Coy, *California County Boundaries: A Study of the Division of the State into Counties and the Subsequent Changes in Their Boundaries* (Berkeley, 1923).

[8] Scientific designation of these groups is more complex. See Alfred L. Kroeber, *Handbook of the Indians of California* (Washington, 1925). Wilson's Tulareños would seem to be partly southern Yokuts and partly of the Serrano division of the Shoshoneans. Some of his Cahuillas were also Serranos, and his Luiseños include the Gabrielino. The original inhabitants of the Santa Barbara-Ventura area were Chumash.

I

The Yumas and Mojaves, who also belong to this district, were never much under mission influence—if at all, as nations—but must be noticed before I conclude. There are no other tribes of much importance, in the present connection.

These six nations (so to call them) inhabit a territory between latitudes 32° 30′ and 35° (or thereabouts,) with an area of about 45,000 square miles. Two-thirds of it is mountain and desert, and not one-half of the rest offers any very strong inducements to attract a dense white population of agriculturists. There are the advantages neither of wood nor of soil and water to tempt American settlers in large numbers farther than sixty or seventy miles from the ocean, even in the most favored county of Los Angeles. Beyond that limit—with the southern line of the State, the rivers Colorado and Mohave, and a line drawn from the last-mentioned river to the Four Creeks (in Tulare county) for its southern, eastern, and northern boundaries—the Government might provide all these Indians with a permanent home.

In such a location under a just system, there is no reason to apprehend an undue pressure of white population upon them, either from the east or the west—at all events, not during the present century.[9]

This is a vital point gained for them, and it removes at the outset one of the principal difficulties which the Government has elsewhere encountered in dealing with Indians. I place it here in the foreground, and have, indeed, expressed myself too cautiously in reference to a territory which needs but a

[9] Superficially it appears that Wilson grossly underestimated the population increase in store for this section of California. Irrigation, mining, mountain and desert resorts, and a network of rail and highway transportation routes have given this region an importance that he did not foresee, but its population is still sparse. As of 1900 there had been very little settlement of this interior region.

glance to know its desolation, compared with the pleasant vales and fertile plains so many of them enjoyed only a few years gone by, along the more level coast.

There, through a distance of 300 miles from San Diego to Santa Ynes, nine parent Missions, and twice as many subordinate establishments were founded, beginning in 1769 and flourished until about 1834, at this date having some fifteen thousand of these people under their protection,[10] and pursuing a successful course of tuition in the arts of civilized life and the duties of morality and religion. In the fall of the Missions—accomplished by private cupidity and political ambition, which too often have wielded the destinies of the poor aborigines—philanthropy laments the failure of one of the grandest experiments ever made for the elevation of this unfortunate race.

It is now the province of our own Government to check the downward career of these children of the Missions, and put them anew in the broad road they followed to happiness, and convey to their brethren who never yet have felt them a taste of the comforts and blessings of civilization. If some one of its various plans of a wise beneficence can be here adapted to their capacity and condition, and the character, pursuits, and prospects of the neighboring white population, of which I entertain no doubt, we may look for the most glorious results, at a day not so remote as to discourage the present exertions of all good men.

There are some general facts proper to be stated in regard to each nation, before venturing upon any specific recom-

[10] The southern missions were the more populous, but 15,000 neophytes is the total for all California in 1834. Hubert Howe Bancroft, *History of California* (7 vols., San Francisco, 1884-1890), III, 356; Sherburne F. Cook, *The Conflict between the California Indian and White Civilization*, I (Berkeley, 1943), 12.

mendations for their management; and strong features of resemblance between them, in their actual condition, which must be carefully kept in view, when we come to judge of the feasibility of such recommendations. I will give the result of my limited experience with them, or of reliable information, with a desire to do them strict justice, and a hope that I may contribute somewhat to their future advancement.

The late Hugo Reid, Esq., a resident here of twenty years, an accomplished scholar, and whose opportunities of knowing the Indians perhaps exceeded those of any other person in the State, wrote some valuable notes and essays upon the languages of the Indians, their ancient customs, and connection with the missions.[11] In his death they have lost a zealous friend, who might have been eminently useful to them at this time. He was of opinion (and so it is generally thought in the country) that the Indians of the South are much more civilized than those in the north, and require an entirely different management.

I. TULAREÑOS

The Tulareños live in the mountain wilderness of the Four Creeks, Porsiuncula (or Kern's or Current) river[12] and the Tejon, and wander thence towards the headwaters of the Mo-

[11] Hugo Reid came to California in 1832. He married Victoria, a daughter of a Gabrielino chief, settled near San Gabriel, and became a prominent citizen in this area. To the Los Angeles *Star*, beginning with the issue of February 21, 1852, he contributed a series of letters on the Indians of Los Angeles County. Several times reprinted, they are most conveniently available in a separate volume edited by Arthur M. Ellis (Los Angeles, 1926), and as an appendix to Susanna Bryant Dakin, *A Scotch Paisano: Hugo Reid's Life in California*, 1832-1852, *Derived from His Correspondence* (Berkeley, 1939).

[12] Kern River, so named after Edward M. Kern of the Frémont expedition, who almost drowned in it, had been christened Río de San Felipe

jave and the neighborhood of the Cahuillas. Their present common name belongs to the Spanish and Mexican times, and is derived from the word *tulare* (a swamp with flags). They were formerly attached to the Missions of Santa Ynes, Santa Barbara, La Purissima, and San Buenaventura, in Santa Barbara county, and San Fernando, in Los Angeles county. They are all of one family: there is very little difference in the languages spoken by the several rancherias (villages).

According to the State census, just completed, there remain 606 Indians "domesticated" in Santa Barbara county—males, 324; females 282; males and females over twenty-one years of age, 364; all, probably, claiming affiliation with the Tulareños. From the same source, we learn that in Tulare county there are 5,800 domesticated Indians (males), and females, 2,600—over twenty-one years of age, 3,787; under twenty-one years, 4,613—the white inhabitants of this county numbering only 174.

They speak the Santa Ynes tongue. In all, 2,000 might be brought at first within the plan I will propose hereafter—to be divided into two pueblos (towns).

There is but one "Mexican claim" upon their land—at the Tejon, of Messrs. Ignacio del Valle and Jose Antonio Aguirre, to eleven square leagues; [13] at least, I have no knowledge of any other.

From the Mohave to the Tejon the distance is about 130 miles; from Los Angeles, 90; from Santa Barbara (say) 70. From the Tejon to Porsiuncula river, 25 miles; and thence to the Four Creeks, 75 miles.

by Father Garcés in 1776 and relabeled Porciúncula by Father Zalvidea in 1806. A better known Porciúncula is the Los Angeles River.

[13] Helen S. Giffen and Arthur Woodward, *The Story of El Tejon* (Los Angeles, 1942).

With greater natural resources than the Cahuillas, San Luiseños, and Dieguiños, yet they often descend upon the ranchos (farms) of Los Angeles and Santa Barbara, carrying back droves of horses, chiefly for food. Sometimes they are caught and shot, or hung, on the spot, as happened in last July to one of their *capitanes* (chiefs); but the same night his men drove off all the horses of a valuable rancho, and in fact, entirely ruined it, for it is not easy to repair the loss of sixty or a hundred horses fit to drive cattle (the loss, I believe, on that occasion). The people suffer severely from this quarter, in the loss of all kinds of stock; and without redress, as these mountain fastnesses almost defy pursuit.[14]

The main southern emigrant route to the San Joaquin passes through this nation; and it is the principal thoroughfare of our rancheros and the upper country drovers during a great part of the year.[15] Their exposure to depredations, in their passage, and even to massacre, is familiar to the Government, in some events of the past two years. In one instance, a citizen of this county, who had been compelled to make an unusual delay at or near the Four Creeks, had a thousand head of cattle taken by the Indians, all of which he lost.[16] It must be understood, however, that they were then excited to a temporary outbreak—fatal to too many citizens! by Indians

[14] For accounts of such depredations see pages 90-97, 146 of this work; Hayes Scrapbooks, Bancroft Library; Robert G. Cleland, *The Cattle on a Thousand Hills* (San Marino, 1941), 90-97; George William Beattie and Helen Pruitt Beattie, *Heritage of the Valley* (Pasadena, 1939), *passim*.

[15] The real basis of southern California prosperity in this period was the delivery of beef to San Francisco and the diggings. One route led through Tejon Pass and the San Joaquin Valley, another by Santa Barbara and the Salinas Valley.

[16] Presumably a trail herd belonging to Henry Dalton. Its loss is described in Lewis Granger to Abel Stearns, Los Angeles, February 4, 1851, Stearns Papers, Huntington Library.

who had fled from the north in consequence of the wars there waged against them by the State Government. With the exception of their frequent forays into the farming country of our lower coast and an occasional restiveness they show along the emigrant and traveled route, they get along peacefully of late.

But these are serious evils, and prove that they demand strict attention, and a respectable military force stationed somewhere between the Tejon and Four Creeks, to keep them in order; even if it be thought that they cannot yet participate in plans that would be expedient with the other nations, an opinion to which I cannot assent.

Under judicious treatment, they will not exhibit fewer of the better qualities of human nature than their neighbors whether Cahuillas, San Luiseños, or Dieguiños.

II. CAHUILLAS

The Cahuillas [17] are a little to the north of the San Luiseños, occupying the mountain ridges and intervening valleys to the east and southeast of Mount San Bernardino, down toward the Mojave river and the desert that borders the river Colorado—the nation of the Mojaves living between them and these rivers. I am unable, just now, to give the number and names of all their villages. San Gorgonio, San Jacinto, Coyote, are among those best known, though others even nearer the desert, are more populous. Agua Caliente was latterly a mixture of Cahuillas and San Luiseños—the connecting link between the two nations, as San Ysidro is considered to be between the former and the Dieguiños. The last chief (proper)

[17] On the Cahuillas, in addition to Kroeber's *Handbook*, see David P. Barrows, *The Ethno-Botany of the Coahuilla Indians of Southern California* (Chicago, 1900).

of Agua Caliente, named Antonio Garra, is said to have been
a Yuma by birth, educated at the Mission of San Luis Rey,
for he could read and write. His appearance was not that of a
Yuma, but there would be nothing strange in finding him "a
man of power" among the Cahuillas or San Luiseños. The
village of San Felipe, about fifteen miles from Agua Caliente,
and always recognized as one of the Dieguiño nation, still
claims to be closely related to, or a branch of, the Yumas; it
uses, however, the Dieguiño language.[18] Agua Caliente, on the
whole, may rather be considered as out of the domain of the
Cahuillas, since its chief was shot and the village destroyed,
about a year ago. I will speak of it, in another connection,
hereafter, as it is of some consequence to these Indians.

The Cahuilla chiefs, and many of the people, speak Spanish. Many still claim to be "Christians;" the majority of them
are not, while the reverse is the case with the San Luiseños
and Dieguiños. A great part of the *neophytes* of San Gabriel,
the wealthiest of the Missions, were Cahuillas. Their name
means "master," in our language, or, as some of them render
it, "the great nation." Their entire number now scarcely ex-
ceeds 3,000 souls.

San Gabriel Mission possessed a valuable establishment on
the present rancho of San Bernardino,[19] the ruined walls of
which, and rows of lofty cottonwoods, with the olives, and
traces of zanjas and fields, remain to attest the noble plans
which the Fathers formed for the benefit of this people. A
large number of them had been gathered here between the
years 1825 and 1834. In the latter year it was destroyed by
the unconverted, and the last tie severed that bound them to

[18] The Yuman and Dieguiño languages belong to the same family.
[19] Established as an *asistencia* in 1819. Beattie, *Heritage of the Valley*,
12-36.

their spiritual conquerors. In the end it might have proved the golden chain of charity, drawing them to a loftier sphere of moral and intellectual existence.

Sometime afterwards, Juan Antonio (whose soubriquet is "General") removed to and kept his village on this rancho, until its purchase last year by a Mormon settlement.[20] He then went fifteen miles further back into the mountains, to San Gorgonio, another old dependency of San Gabriel, leaving the Mormons in quiet possession of almost a principality capable of sustaining a working population of 50,000 souls. They employ and cultivate the kindliest relations with all the Indians, and I am happy to state, never permit ardent spirits to be sold or given to them.

At San Gorgonio the Indians are brought into contact with Mr. Pauline Weaver,[21] who claims to have a Mexican title, but, notoriously, without any regular, written grant. The heirs of José Antonio Estudillo claim the rancho of San Jacinto, the site of another of their villages. The first claims three square leagues; the last eleven square leagues, more or less.[22] Both were minor Mission establishments. They are about eighty miles from the city of Los Angeles. In Mt. San Bernardino there is a single mill-site, claimed by Mr. Luis Vignes,[23] as lessee of the Mexican Government for five years, I believe; now occupied in his name by Mr. Daniel Sexton.[24]

[20] On the Mormons at San Bernardino consult Hallock F. Raup, *San Bernardino, California: Settlement and Growth of a Pass-Site City* (Berkeley, 1940), and Beattie, *Heritage of the Valley*, 170-310.

[21] A mountaineer, guide, and prospector of some fame. He and Isaac Williams had petitioned the Mexican authorities in 1845 for title to this former mission rancho. Beattie, *Heritage of the Valley*, 58, 68.

[22] Approximately 13,000 and 50,000 acres.

[23] Vignes is better known as a pioneer vintner. His mill gave the name to Mill Creek Canyon.

[24] A Californian since 1841.

The Cahuillas have not had a head-chief, I believe, since the death of the one they called "Razon" (White). He died within two or three years past, at an advanced age. They gave him his name, as they told me, from his always acting so much like a white man, in staying at home and tending his fields and flocks, for he had both. When a young man, he went off to Sonora (under what circumstances, is not known), and returned a farmer—which is all the early history we have of him. He was always a quiet, good, industrious man, and rendered material service to the authorities, in arresting the half-civilized Indian outlaws who have sometimes fled with stolen horses to the mesquit wilds of his village. Cabezon, too, is a good old Indian chief, as also another named Juan Bautista.

Juan Antonio, however, has a more conspicuous figure among them, by a sort of iron energy which he often displays, and is better known to the whites. A passing comment upon some of his acts may not be out of place, as they touch the present subject.

In the summer of 1851, the local authorities deemed it expedient to conciliate him with a hundred dollars' worth of cloth, hats, and handkerchiefs—not beads—paid for out of the County Treasury. This present seems to have been the winding up of the following incident. A while before, he had killed eleven Americans, who were accused of robbing the aforesaid rancho of San Bernardino, where he then had his village. He claimed to be justified by an order of a Justice of the Peace, one of the proprietors of the rancho, whose house, it was alleged, the Americans were rifling at the time of the Indian attack.[25] A perfect uproar ensued in the county, and

[25] For description of Juan Antonio's campaign against John Irving and his gang of San Francisco and Sydney outlaws, as well as the subsequent repercussions, see Beattie, *Heritage of the Valley*, 84-89; *History of San Bernardino County* (San Francisco, Wallace W. Elliott and Company,

the Indians fled to the mountains, not, however, without offering battle to a company of fifty volunteers then stationed
near the scene, who were equally anxious to punish the massacre of their countrymen in this unauthorized manner. The
exertions of their commanding officer, the late Major General
J. H. Bean, restrained them (not without difficulty), and thus
prevented a general war, which must have proved for a time
disastrous to the settlements.

Such a precedent is too dangerous for repetition. Doubtless, the Indians thought they were only acting in obedience
to the authorities, it having been the custom, in the Mexican
times, to employ them in services of this kind; and, I have
reason to believe, something like it has been done recently in
killing two Sonoranians, undoubtedly horse thieves. The necessity for correcting their ideas on this subject, is evident. I
mean, of course, that they ought never to be allowed to med-
dle with the punishment of whites for public offences.

Juan Antonio gained a less perilous celebrity, in the winter
of 1851, for his successful stratagem in capturing the Antonio
Garra before mentioned, and putting an end to his conspiracy
for the general massacre of the American inhabitants along
the coast.[26] This gave rise to a treaty of peace.[27] Permit me to

1883), 77-79; Los Angeles *Star*, June 7, 1851, and November 20, 1851,
Hayes, Scrapbooks, XXXVIII, Bancroft Library.

[26] Antonio Garrá, chief of the Cahuillas at Warner's Ranch, plotted a
general Indian uprising which alarmed all southern California. San Diego
mustered every able-bodied man in an emergency army, the Mormons
at San Bernardino stockaded themselves, and Los Angeles put in the
field a ranger company under Joshua H. Bean. It was Juan Antonio, however, who went down with twenty-five of his warriors and arrested Garrá.
See Beattie, *Heritage of the Valley*, 184-89; Los Angeles *Star*, January 17,
1852, Hayes Scrapbooks, XXXVIII.

[27] A treaty of peace, amity, and friendship, executed by General J. H.
Bean, and reported in the Los Angeles *Star*, January 3, 1852.

observe that this document means something or nothing—in the latter case, is worse than idle. The Indians, in their own unsophisticated logic, have ascribed *some* effect to it. On the part of the State, it is at least a *guarantee of their title* to a very large territory.

Like a "treaty" made since,[28] purporting to be with a larger number of the same and other Indians, and aiming at a wider scope of operations (and not yet fulfilled), it may have given them the most erroneous notions of themselves, and of their true relations to the people and the Government. Vanity may do them awhile, but anon they will clamor for the promised *beef!* Seriously, there should be no tampering with these, nor any Indians, by promises of high sound, that cannot be executed to the letter. This last mentioned appears to have been hurried through in a spirit of wild speculation, wholly regardless of the interests either of the Government or the Indians.

These very "treaties" and some of the incidents alluded to above, furnish weighty reasons for infusing a new vigor into the national policy in this quarter, that shall go right to the root of the evil under which whites and Indians alike are now suffering.

[It may not be improper here to digress from the main object of the report, to insert a note which we find attached to the manuscript as an appendix, referring to a letter of the late Hugo Reid:][29]

[28] Negotiated by O. M. Wozencraft, one of the federal Indian commissioners, with the Cahuillas, and the Indians of Agua Caliente, Temecula, and elsewhere. It set up an Indian territory about thirty miles by forty, between San Gorgonio and Warner's Ranch. Along with some seventeen other treaties with California Indians this one failed of ratification in the United States Senate. For the text see 32 Cong., 1 sess., *Message from the President of the United States, Communicating Eighteen Treaties Made with the Indians of California.*

[29] Note by the editor of the *Star.*

Soon after the settlement of San Antonio, the establishment of San Gabriel was determined on, and missionaries with soldiers were dispatched from San Diego for that purpose. The following is the miraculous account given of this expedition by Father Palou:

"On the 10th of August, the Father Friar Pedro Cambon, and Father Angel Somera, guarded by ten soldiers, with the muleteers and beasts requisite to carry the necessaries, set out from San Diego, and traveled northerly by the same route as the former expedition for Monterey had gone. After proceeding about forty leagues, they arrived at the river Temblores; and while they were in the act of examining the ground in order to fix a proper place for the mission, a multitude of Indians, all armed and headed by two captains, presented themselves, setting up horrid yells, and seeming determined to oppose the establishment of the mission. The Fathers, fearing that war would ensue, took out a piece of cloth with the image of our Lady de los Dolores, and held it up to the view of the barbarians. This was no sooner done than the whole were quiet, being subdued by the sight of this most precious image; and throwing on the ground their bows and arrows, the two captains came running with great haste to lay the beads which they brought about their necks at the feet of the sovereign queen, as a proof of their entire regard; manifesting at the same time that they wished to be at peace with us. They then informed the whole of the neighborhood of what had taken place; and the people in large numbers, men, women, and children, soon came to see the holy virgin, bringing food, which they put before her, thinking she required to eat, as others. In this manner the gentiles of the mission of San Gabriel were so entirely changed that they frequented the establishment without reserve, and hardly knew how much to manifest their pleasure that the Spaniards had come to settle in their country. Under these favorable auspices, the Fathers proceeded to found the mission with the accustomed ceremonies, and celebrated the first mass under a tree on the nativity of the Virgin, the eighth of September, 1771."[30]

Mr. Reid's view of the conversion at San Gabriel is "as related by the old Indians." Even in the mountains, and far on the sandy deserts of California, I have observed Indians cross themselves and appear to say their prayers at night, when they could not know that the eye of man was upon them. How far their theological knowledge goes, it is difficult to tell. The simple Fathers seem to have thought that there was a profound philosophy, and nearly all of religion, in that sublime idea, "Love God"—"*Amará Dios.*"

There may have been a degree of force used with some refractory village, but if we are to understand the text to mean that this was general, the "old Indians," who gave Mr. Reid his information have a very different version from that of historical narratives left to us.

The second San Diego mission was destroyed, and one of the Fathers killed, by the wild Indians, in 1775, instigated by two renegade neophytes. The Viceroy only seconded the wishes of the founder (Junipero Serra) when he ordered the ringleaders to be released without punishment, and the Indians to be treated with even greater kindness and condescension; this being the most proper way "to pacificate their minds and reduce the neighboring gentiles."[31] The good Junipero ascribed it all to their want of knowledge and "*el influjo del*

[30] Translated from Francisco Palou, *Relación histórica de la vida y apostólicas tareas del venerable padre fray Junípero Serra* (Mexico, 1787), 130–31.

[31] This quotation and those that follow are from Palou, *Relación histórica.*

infernal enemigo." It was re-founded about two years afterwards, with the aid of twelve soldiers, "to the great pleasure
of the Indians, the neophytes working with much joy," etc.
There seems to have been this charge of "force" among some
of the wild rancherias, because sixty had been baptized in a
single day.

The same year (1777) with ten soldiers and a corporal, and
neophytes from San Gabriel, Junipero built up San Juan
Capistrano. "As an interpreter from San Gabriel enabled him
at once to explain his object in coming to live among them,
which was to teach them the road to heaven, make them Christians that they might be saved, etc., so well did they understand and become impressed, that the natives here instantly
began to ask for baptism; whilst those of the other missions
molested the Fathers for something to eat and other presents,
these of San Juan Capistrano molested them for baptism, of
their own accord lengthening out the hours of instruction."

An image of the Virgin—not the musket—first moved the
Gabrielenos! And they were "so changed by the sight of it,
that, in their frequent visits to the Fathers, they did not know
how to prove their content that the latter had become neighbors on their lands; the gentiles cut the greater part of the
wood for and helped to build the houses, whence the Fathers
hoped for a happy result, and that from that moment they
would not refuse the sweet yoke of the evangelical law." There
were only sixteen soldiers here. The rash act of one of them
disturbed this harmony for awhile, but the efforts of the Fathers "with all suavity to draw to them" the Indians, soon
banished the memory of the soldier's wrong, and they "began to present their children for baptism."

In 1784 this mission had 1,019 converts, San Diego 1,060,
and San Juan 472; and all the missions, at the same date (Au-

gust 28th) had 5,080, and on the last day of said year, 6,736.
I quote from the"Life of Father Junipero Serra," [32] published
at Mexico, 1787, which is full of touching passages illustra-
tive of the mild and inoffensive character of the aboriginal
Californians, and not less of the unaffected piety of the ad-
venturous missionaries who sought honestly, all will admit,
even if they did not completely effect, their conversion. San
Diego, San Juan, and San Gabriel, in 1784, had a majority of
all the neophytes. San Buenaventura was then just founded,
with perhaps a hundred neophytes; the rest of the southern
missions were established afterwards. It was the boast of the
eulogists of Junipero, that he left at his death, in the last mentioned year, after fifteen years of labor, six settlements of
Spaniards established in California,[33] and nine purely of native neophytes.

III. SAN LUISEÑOS AND DIEGUIÑOS

For the purposes of this report, the San Luiseños and Dieguiños may be considered as one nation, understanding and
speaking habitually each other's language, having both been
more generally christianized than the other nations and more
intimately connected with the whites. They are a large majority of the laborers, mechanics, and servants of San Diego
and Los Angeles counties. Obviously, their present distinctive
names are derived from their respective missions, namely San
Luis Rey and San Diego. Nearly all speak the Spanish language, and some of the chiefs read and write it. The two na-

[32] A want ad for this volume, by "a gentleman who is preparing a history of California from the earliest date," ran for several months in the
latter part of 1852 in the Los Angeles *Star*.

[33] The presidios of San Diego, Santa Barbara, Monterey, and San Francisco, and the pueblos of San Jose and Los Angeles.

tions together are estimated at 5,000 souls, a majority of whom are within the limits of this State.

The villages of the San Luiseños are in a section of country adjacent to the Cahuillas, between forty and seventy miles in the mountainous interior from San Diego; they are known as Las Floras, Santa Margarita, San Luis Rey Mission, Wahoma, Pala, Temecula, Alhuanga (two villages), La Joya, Potrero, and Bruno's and Pedro's villages within five or six miles of Agua Caliente; they are all in San Diego county.

The villages of the Dieguiños, wherever they live separately, are a little further to the south. Indeed, under this appellation, they extend a hundred miles into Lower California, in about an equal state of civilization, and thence are scattered through the Tecate Valley, over the entire desert on the west side of New River. Far on the east side, among the dreary sandhills that form the barrier there [are] the wilder Yumas. Until very lately the Dieguiños have suffered much from the hostility of a populous and warlike village called Yacum, near the mouth of the river Colorado. They are thought to be diminishing in numbers more rapidly than the other nations.

Their villages (known to me) are San Dieguito (about 20 souls), San Diego Mission (20), San Pasqual (75), Camajal (two villages, 100), Santa Ysabel (100), San Jose (100), Matahuay (75), Lorenzo (30), San Felipe (100), Cajon (40), Cuyamaca (50), Valle de los Viejos (50). These numbers are given from information believed to be correct.

Pablo Assis, Chief of Temecula, claims one and a half leagues at that place, under a written grant; and a claim to the rancho of Temecula is preferred by Mr. Louis Vignes. Eight other of their village sites are claimed by different persons—San Jose, if I mistake not, by two opposite "claims," that of Mr. J. J. Warner, and Portilla, amounting to four square leagues. The claim of Mr. Vignes, at Temecula, amounts to eight square leagues. Agua Caliente is also claimed by Mr. J. J. Warner.

From the city of Los Angeles to Temecula is 80 miles; thence to Agua Caliente, 35 miles.

The languages of the Dieguiños and Yumas bear a strong analogy to each other, if, indeed, they are not one and the same language. The opinion of Don Juan Bandini, whose opportunities of knowing them have been ample, is that their language is the same.

GENERAL OBSERVATIONS

Associated with the Cahuillas may sometimes be found the Serranos; and the Indians of San Juan Capistrano with the San Luiseños. I am not prepared to say that the two former are not the same people, to all intents and purposes, at this day. Mr. Reid has located the Serranos along the upper waters of the Santa Ana river, and between the Los Angeles county Indians (whom he calls Gabrielinos) and the Cahuillas. Some of the Serrano women are good seamstresses. The Indians of San Juan—the finest of the south in appearance, temper, and intellect—are now nearly extinct, from intermarriage with the Spaniards and other more usual causes of Indian decay. Very few of the Gabrielinos are to be met with here now. "A few," says Mr. Reid, "are to be found at San Fernando, San Gabriel, and Los Angeles. Those in service on ranchos are a mere handful. You will find at present more of them in the county of Monterey than in this, excluding the three places named above. Death has been busy among them for years past, and very few more are wanting, to extinguish the lamp which God lighted. The Indians from the

northwest coast killed great numbers, years ago, on the is-
lands" (San Clemente and Santa Catalina).[34]

The three or four prominent nations that remain, as above
described, have different languages and a different physical
appearance, in some respects. How far the Cahuilla and San
Luiseño tongues resemble each other, is a subject worthy of
investigation; and Mr. Reid would no doubt have thrown
much light upon it, if he had lived to carry out his inquiries.
The Tulareños, Cahuillas, and San Luiseños are universally
understood to have distinct original languages; but their common knowledge of the Spanish tongue forms their usual means
of communication. The use of the last has tended to make
them forget the original language. Individuals of the same nation, as a habit, talk with each other in Spanish, seemingly,
in preference to the native tongue; often, of course, it must
be from necessity, in the poverty of the native tongue, or having forgotten it.

"The languages of San Luis Rey and San Juan Capistrano
bear a strong analogy." I quote a manuscript of Mr. Reid's,
which I am kindly permitted to use. "When we come to San
Buenaventura, Santa Barbara, San Ynes, and La Purissima,
we find not only a distinct language, but a strongly marked
difference in their color and physical appearance, the southern Indians being red, while the others here mentioned are a
very dark hue, stronger set in their limbs, although less powerful and very diminutive in stature. Some of the young Indian girls about San Gabriel and San Fernando are of a pleas-
ing countenance, well-formed features, and, in many cases,
of a light complexion, which is not caused by admixture of
blood. Females to the north are of coarse features, and even

34 *The Indians of Los Angeles County*, ed. Arthur M. Ellis, 67-68.

blacker than the men. I have been acquainted with the lodges up and down the coast for years and never recollect of seeing a fair skinned female, without the blood had been mixed. This has arisen, no doubt, from their living principally on the sea-coast. Arriving as high as Monterey, we again find the Indians of the same color and appearance as those in Los Angeles and San Diego, but with another distinct language. In the San Gabriel language there is a total absence of 'l'—it abounds in the Santa Ynes." [35]

In Santa Barbara, Los Angeles, and San Diego counties, there are nearly 7,000 Indians, excluding the Yumas and Mojaves, and few petty tribes. Not half as many as the neophytes alone left by the Mission! Still, more than half of those we have are the survivors of the Missions.

That they are corrupt, and becoming more so every day, no candid man can dispute. They do not always find better examples to imitate now than they saw in the past generation of whites; for the latter have not improved in the social virtues as fast as the Indians have declined. What marvel that eighteen years of neglect, misrule, oppression, slavery, and injustice, and every opportunity and temptation to gratify their natural vices withal, should have given them a fatal tendency downward to the very lowest degradation!

Not to dwell further upon whatever differences a people so situated may have in appearance or language, let us follow up, rather, the circumstances and analogies that may lead them to accommodate themselves to some common system of Governmental benevolence.

These will more fully appear from a view of the actual condition in which we find them, as domesticated laborers and

[35] For other writings by the same author see the Reid Manuscripts, Los Angeles County Museum.

servants, as land proprietors, or in their mountain villages—
in their individual and national capacity. I am not certain that
the word "domesticated" does not apply to all of them, with
a certain degree of propriety; certainly, it may be so applied
to the great mass of the Dieguiños, San Luiseños, Cahuillas,
and of the Tulareños coming within the scope of my objects
in the present report.

THE LABORERS AND SERVANTS

The Indian laborers and servants are "domesticated;" mix
with us daily and hourly; and, with all their faults, appear to
be a necessary part of the domestic economy. They are almost
the only house or farm servants we have. The San Luiseño is
the most sprightly, skillful, and handy; the Cahuilla plodding,
but strong, and very useful with instruction and watching.

When at work, they will do without ardent spirits, but *must*
have it on Saturday night and Sunday. Very little of the money
earned during the week goes for meat and bread—their chief
want with it is for drink and cards.[36] They are universal gamblers, and inveterately addicted to the vice; consequently,
their clothing continually changes hands. Yet, I have met with
some who do not drink, and have an aspiration to decency.
Some, again, are idle and vagabonds; but I have rarely found
them unwilling to work, when well paid.

If it be true that they cannot do half the work a white man
can, 'tis equally true that custom at best never allows them
more than half the wages of the latter, and, generally, much
less than half. The common pay of Indian farm hands is from
eight to ten dollars per month; and one dollar per day the

---

[36] The week-end craving for strong drink had been acquired since the
coming of the whites; the addiction to gambling dated back to the days
before the Spaniards. Kroeber, *Handbook*, 846-50.

highest in the towns—but few pay so much. No white man here, whether American, Sonoranian, or Californian, will work for such wages, nor anything like it.

That better wages merely would make the Indian here a better man, is doubtful. With more money, he would only pursue his evil tastes to greater excess. When their weekly *juegos* (plays) were restrained by the magistrates, and only allowed at distant intervals they were much better off; and then, too, liquor shops were not so common. In some streets of this little city, almost every other house is a grog-shop for Indians. They have, indeed, become sadly deteriorated, within the last two years; and it may be long, very long, before a sound public opinion will speak like the potent voice of the Mission Fathers.

But, let us remember, these same Indians built all the houses in the country, and planted all the fields and vineyards. There is hardly any sort of ordinary work for which they do not show a good-will.

Under the Missions, they were masons, carpenters, plasterers, soap-makers, tanners, shoemakers, blacksmiths, millers, bakers, cooks, brick-makers, carters and cart-makers, weavers and spinners, saddlers, shepherds, agriculturists, horticulturists, viñeros, vaqueros—in a word, filled all the laborious occupations known to civilized society. Their work must have been rudely executed sometimes, it may well be supposed; and they have forgotten much they once knew. But they acquired the rudiments of a practical knowledge which has outlived their good teachers, and contributed much to the little improvement this section of country has reached in eighteen years.

They are inferior only to the American in bodily strength, and might soon rank with the best Californian and Sonoranian in all the arts necessary to their physical comfort. They teach the American, even, how to make an adobe (sun-dried brick), mix the *lodo* (mud mortar), put on the *brea* (pitch) for roof—all these, recondite arts to the new beginner, yet very important to be known, when there are no other building materials. They understand the mysteries of irrigation, the planting season, and the harvest. Poor unfortunates! they seldom have farms of their own to till, or a dwelling to shelter them from the rain!

Such is the laborer and servant, of no matter what nation. A spendthrift, but willing to work, if paid; never a beggar, save when old age or infirmity has overtaken him; humble, without servility; skilled in a great many useful things; yet full of vices, I am afraid, because he has so few encouragements to virtue. He always adheres to the truth, cost what it may; still, many are petty thieves.

The women have not forgotten their needlework, as may be noticed at any time; they dress in the common Spanish style of this country, and always make their own garments. Like the men, they are much addicted to intemperance; hearty, good humored creatures, yet with a great aversion to regular work. I refer to those about the towns.

As a general thing, the women are quick to learn the various household duties. There are striking examples of Indian women, married to foreigners and native Californians, exemplary wives and mothers.

IV. A HASTY GLANCE AT THE LAND PROPRIETORS

At the close of the late Mexican war, some of the old Mission Indians remained in possession of tracts of land, which they had held for a long time by occupancy and license of the Fathers, or under written grants from the Mexican Government.

Some have since sold out, for trivial considerations—others have been elbowed off by white neighbors; so that, in the settled and settling parts of the country, there are not now fifty Indian land proprietors. They are awaiting the adjudication of the Commissioners of Land Titles. A league is the largest tract any of them claim; in general, their tracts do not exceed fifty or a hundred acres.

Many of them are good citizens, in all respects, except the right to vote and be witnesses in the State courts, where others than their own race are concerned. They are anxious to hold on to their little homesteads, and resist all offers to buy as steadily as they can. How long their limited shrewdness can match the over-reaching cupidity that ever assails them, is difficult to say. They lack thrift and prudent management, and are strongly inclining to dissolute habits; though they plant regularly from year to year. Some have a small stock of horses, cows, and sheep.

A better crop and more commodious hut—perhaps, a table and chair or two—may distinguish them from the denizens of the mountain village. Everything else is quite after the Indian fashion. Still, with these, and the right to land, and honest conduct, they have made a broad step towards civilization.

Were they in villages, and had they *there* the powerful hand of Government to guide and protect them, their example might do some good; as it is, they serve in no way to benefit their race, while there is too much danger that, with all their bright promise, they may be drawn themselves in the vortex that swallows up the hopes of their brethren who hire out on the farms or crowd around the cities.

They now have a little capital, which might be turned to account by a faithful trustee or true guardian. Speculation, lawsuits, fraud, and force will soon wring it from their open hands, in all probability.

To the Missions they can never go again, with hope of finding a home. The successors of the Fathers are there, for a priest
is stationed at all except two, I believe. Any Sunday, a few Indians may still be seen near the altar, summoned by the chimes
that once pealed over a smiling multitude gathered for wor-
ship, or the harmless diversions wherein their happy hours
passed away. These are all, and they seem serious and rever-
ent at the church. The rest linger there in their straggling huts
of brush or tule, trying to get a meagre subsistence out of the
small patches not yet taken up by the whites—ill-clothed, in
filth and wretchedness, without food half the year, save what
is stolen. If there be "savages" among these southern Indians,
a Mission is now the place to seek them, where riot and debauchery reign supreme. This is notorious to good citizens
who have settled around them, but the violence of the reckless and unprincipled bids defiance to restraint, at present. I
am not certain that some of the Indians do not preserve a
sort of vague belief that these immense buildings, to our eye
greatly dilapidated and fast going to ruin, yet, with their rude
repairs, ample enough for their accommodation, are ultimately to be restored to them. It is no exaggeration to repeat that
the Indians lurking about the Missions, with an occasional
exception, are the worst in the country, morally speaking; and
the sooner they are removed, the better for all concerned.

Within the last two years, the Indians have had a very per-
ceptible tendency towards returning permanently to a mountain life, in spite of its forbidding aspect.[37]

They began by deserting the larger ranchos for the freer

[37] A contributor to the Los Angeles *Star*, in August, 1852, complained
that the federal policy of making presents to the Indians through their
tribal leaders accelerated this tendency and had "led to the abandonment
of the ranchos and pueblos by the Indians almost entirely," thereby de-
priving town and country of valuable laborers. See pp. 75-77 of this work.

indulgences of the city and the grog-shops at the Missions, where they could have their famous and favorite *juegos*. The complaint had been universal on this subject. Many have thus become habitual drinkers, who used to be content with their allowances upon the ranchos—for custom has always allowed them ardent spirits, from which lamentable practice not even the Missions can be excepted. Yet the wonder is, with some, how these Indians have become such drunkards! The laws of nature have had their course, as usual, and the Indian is paying the penalty exacted of all who violate them.

Unfitted—many of them—for hard work, by drinking and their games, (they have been known to die from the violent exertions required by some of these,) [38] ashamed or afraid to go back to their old *amos* (masters), uncared for by strangers, in some way taught to dislike *los Americanos*, and restive under all the neglect they suffer; having caught the idea that they are free, (three years ago they were practically slaves,) with none to teach them the true hopes and duties of freemen, and finding, with the long experiment, that American freedom does not profit them—some such motives, I suppose, may drive them to enjoy the old and kindred associations of their tribe, where they are sure to meet a warm friendship and a hospitality generous in its extremest poverty. Hospitality I know to be one of their virtues.

On the other hand, as the young men of the mountains grow up, the cravings of hunger, or a love of novelty, carry them to the towns in quest of employment, or to gratify curiosity. They soon fall into the bad ways of their "Christian"

[38] Their all-night sessions at *peon*, the guessing game, were doubtless hard on the constitution, but physical breakdown and death from over-exertion stemmed rather from the violence of their variant of shinny and the ball game, a cross country race in which each contestant kicked along a small ball.

relations, and return a little worse for the visit. If they have chanced, in their "rounds," to have met with the marshal and jailor, or their Indian "deputies," (alcaldes, in common parlance,) they could have fared better anywhere else in the wide world; and well may they return disgusted with their prospects in civilized life, if they are capable of thinking at all. The Indian has a quick sense of injustice; he can comprehend it when it is plain and very brutal. He can never see why he is sold out to service an indefinite period for intemperance, while the white man goes unpunished for the same thing, and the very richest, or best men, to his eye, are such as tempt him to drink, and sometimes will pay him for his labor in no other way. I am speaking now frankly of abuses which actually exist—not the fair result of the State law, which is a pretty good one, in regard to this point, but cannot be enforced, for the simple reason that the Indians themselves are not allowed to be witnesses as to breaches of it, except for or against each other.

The abuses of the law have been cruel and injurious to the Indian, in every country, and at all times; how nearly fatal to him in California!

Let us follow them, then, to

THE MOUNTAIN VILLAGES.

The best of them, much as they have mixed with the whites, or may know of labor and property, yet love to visit and revisit the rancherias. Tradition preserves a remembrance of things they delight to tell of; Christianity has been far from extinguishing their ancient superstitions and customs. Let a "Christian" set his mind upon seeing his *parientes* (relations) at Temecula or San Gorgonio, no friendship, nor work undone, nor reasonable sum of money, will keep him with you.

In the wilder mountain villages they lead pretty much the same course of life their fathers did eighty years ago, when the Spanish soldier first trampled their grass fields and flower beds. On the coast, however, the supply of food must have been more plentiful, as the sea afforded so many varieties of fish; but since, they have learned to cultivate wheat.

Their present country may be described as a series of low mountain ridges, a few peaks covered with snow in winter, having numerous valleys, generally small but very fertile, which little streams irrigate, that do not run far before they lose themselves in the sand. In the valleys they have their villages. Sometimes all their water is from isolated springs that do not run, or from holes dug in the sand. A great portion of such a country produces no vegetation at all. Other parts give their favorite mezquite bean and acorn, the pine nut, tuna (fruit of cactus), maguey, mescal, berries and seeds of grass and herbs, all of which, with a moderate culture of wheat, corn, melons, and pumpkins, and various small animals, form their staple food. The Cahuillas are not fond of bear meat, and have no deer to hunt; the Dieguiños and San Luiseños have no bear, but hunt the deer and antelope, the former abounding upon their hills and vales. They manufacture very useful blankets, a kind of urn to hold water and keep it cool in summer (called *olla*), a sweat-cloth for the saddle, from the maguey fibre, called a *coco*, etc.[39]

Such is the country, and such the actual resources, of these four nations, in their wilder state. Yet, in this dreary wilderness, God gave them land enough for their comfortable subsistence. But, of that presently. In bad seasons, as things now stand, they are often half starved. They are prodigal, too, by

[39] Compare with Barrows' description of their material culture in *The Ethno-Botany of the Coahuilla Indians*. Aboriginally they did no planting and had no animal husbandry.

nature and by custom. At their annual feast, which always takes place soon after harvest, I have seen them dancing around a large fire, in honor of a deceased relation, and end the ceremony by throwing into the flames their entire stock of provisions and clothing. I have reason to believe that their imprudence and want of forethought frequently lead to death by starvation, especially in cases of sickness.

Juan Antonio frequently calls home his followers; and at any time, such is the subordination among them, all, except the old and sick, would permanently leave the settlements, upon a summons from their respective chiefs. I should, also, include the land proprietors in the exception, and some others who may have a peculiar devotion to certain families. And the same, I believe, may be said safely of the chiefs of villages belonging to other nations.

The present chiefs, in general, understand their affairs very well, and appear to be keenly alive to the good of their people. They often come to the towns—to this city, at any rate—and inflict some punishment in particular cases, the merits of which are left to be "best known to themselves." They exercise a sort of patriarchal supervision over the domesticated, as well as the wilder classes of the nation. I do not wish to convey the idea that they have any regular government, or system of law, or rational grades of punishment, much less that they indulge in very refined distinctions as to guilt. Murder and witchcraft (when it results fatally!) are punished with death. And it is probable, if the local authorities here should ask it, as a favor, the chiefs would shoot, hang, or bury alive (for this they do sometimes) any notorious horse-thief or cattle-stealer.[40] The popular influence ought to be very strong,

[40] Indian chiefs not uncommonly were willing to punish culprits or to surrender them for punishment. See pages 96-97 of this work.

on the other hand, if we may credit the excuse given by Antonio Garra for his attack on Warner's house in 1851; namely, that "he did not want to make the attack then, but his people forced him to go, and he followed." The people have been known to punish by a prompt exercise of authority; and 'tis certain, that considerable respect is always paid to them.

The chiefs of the Cahuillas, San Luiseños, and Dieguiños have shown a commendable spirit in restraining their people from cattle-stealing in Los Angeles and San Diego counties. Thefts of this kind are not as common as might be expected from their necessities and the opportunities they would have for concealment. The crime is common, indeed; but it is notorious to every cattle owner that these Indians have in it little "act or part," compared with a certain class of the settled population.[41] Yet it does occur, occasionally, among the Indians, with all their indisposition to provoke a war with the whites; and will occur, so long as the present equivocal and unjust relations continue to exist between them, and this kind of property ranges over an area of 1,000 square miles, unguarded and with an utter impossibility of being guarded. The temptation is too great for a hungry Indian.

THE MOUNTAIN VILLAGES.

Radically, even the Tulareños, a portion of whom commit greater depredations, are not disposed, as a people, to hostility towards the whites. Individual acts of robbery, however, are apt to recoil upon the whole nation; and rightly enough, when their chiefs refuse to surrender the wrong-doers. But the Tulareños, like the others, always do this upon demand;

[41] The news reports of the period support this contention, placing far more blame upon white marauders, Sonoran, Californian, and American, and upon Indian raiders from more distant tribes.

as happened not many months since, in the delivery of two murderers (Indians) by a chief from the vicinity of Tejon. Another illustration this of an idea I wish always to be kept in mind, touching all these Mission Indians; namely, that they have a common spirit of amity for the whites, and that their general inclination is not for war. They want peace with the whites.

Between the Ttulareños and the others, there is very little intercourse; but, likewise, no existing enmity. The Cahuillas, who are the nearest, are separated from the former by a waste of barren ridges, at a distance of eighty miles or more. Of all these nations it may be said, notwithstanding a little coolness now and then, an individual broil, or even a sudden temporary outbreak between two or more rancherias, nothing happens among them that may be likened at all to a state of war, or to that fixed and lasting jealousy and inveterate hatred ever renewing the strife, as between the Sioux and Chippewas, for example, or the former and the Pawnees.[42]

Their national plays and festivals, gaming, drinking, wandering from place to place, and visiting relatives—these are their principal excitements, not war. They are at peace with one another.

This must be esteemed a very important feature in their relations. It augurs well for any efforts the Government may resolve to make towards their farther amelioration. It may be a powerful motive to that end, since it proves how easily, under the extremest goadings of neglect and injury, and in the final effort of despair and want, they might all be combined against our scattered settlements.

The Yumas, too, and the Mojaves—so far as we have any information of them—are friendly with these nations. There

[42] An observation fully substantiated. See Kroeber, *Handbook*, passim.

is hardly any room for doubt that the former were in perfect concert with Antonio Garra, in his insurrection before mentioned. And having spoken of this event once more, I ought to say that it grew immediately out of the collection of the State taxes from the San Luiseños and Cahuillas, in part; they were also misled by their confidential advisers, unintentionally on the part of the latter, I am willing to believe. It was an extraordinary measure to have taxed Indians at all, in their present condition, who can so much better receive than give.

I have aimed neither to exaggerate nor underrate the qualities of these nations. Viewed as a mass, whether in their individual or their national capacity, they exhibit in common the traits which are always looked to as the groundwork of a rapid civilization.

They are devoted neither to war nor the chase; they have learned to labor for subsistence; they have acquired the idea of separate property in land; they possess a considerable skill in the useful arts; they are at peace among themselves, and friendly to the whites—docile and tractable, and accustomed to subjection.

Had they come into the hands of the American Government when they left the Missions, who can doubt that they would now be the equals, at least, of the Choctaws and Cherokees? If they cannot be made to advance as rapidly, then is all history a fable, and philanthropy an empty dream.

A plan for their benefit may be considered under two heads: first, their territory; second, their management.

TERRITORY.

I would propose for the western line of the Indian Territory (the other lines having been mentioned already,) a line drawn from the eastern boundary of Santa Isabela Rancho, or its neighborhood, direct to the northeastern corner of the Laguna Rancho (thereby including Temecula and Agua Caliente); thence along the northern boundary of Laguna, so as to include the San Jacinto Rancho and the tract commonly known by the name of San Gorgonio—the whole distance (say) 100 miles; thence in a direct course, (say) 120 miles, to the Tejon, including the rancho of that name; thence (say) 100 miles, to the Four Creeks; the rest of this line to be completed by running due south (say) 40 miles, from Santa Isabela to the boundary line between Mexico and the United States. It would have to be remembered that through this territory pass the main routes of travel and emigration, one of which, along the Tejon and Four Creeks, has been mentioned. Another leads from Los Angeles, by the Mormon settlement of San Bernardino, Cajon Pass, and Mojave River, to Salt Lake and New Mexico; [43] another from Los Angeles, by Temecula and Agua Caliente, (intersecting here the main road from San Diego) to New River and the mouth of the Gila. [44] There is a more southern, nearer, and better route [45] from San Diego to the mouth of the Gila, going for the most part immediately along the boundary between the United States and Mexico. These are all good wagon roads, or can be made so; and the country from the Mojave to the Four Creeks and San Joaquin is passable with wagons on one route.

[43] The trail from Salt Lake was outlined by Jedediah Smith as early as 1826 and began to have important traffic in 1849. Traders used the New Mexico route in 1829 and emigrants in 1841. See Joseph J. Hill, "The Old Spanish Trail," *Hispanic American Historical Review*, IV (1922), 444-73; William L. Manly, *Death Valley in '49* (San Jose, 1894); John Walton Caughey, "Southwest from Salt Lake in 1849," *Pacific Historical Review*, VI (1937), 143-64.

[44] Subsequently employed by the overland stages.

[45] Shorter, but not better.

The respective limits of the nations could be defined as conveniently as counties are elsewhere—indeed, there are natural and obvious boundaries—and the Indians would all readily acquiesce in any common sense arrangement. Mount San Bernardino being of importance to the settlers, on account of its pine timber, the northern boundary of the Cahuillas might be placed to the south and east of it, instead of to the north; in such case, the main western line of the Indian Territory, as first set forth above, would be entirely north of Mount San Bernardino and the Cajon Pass, leaving the space of (say) 100 miles between the Cahuillas and Tulareños, wholly unoccupied by any of these Indians, and giving the white inhabitants pine to last them a thousand year, (and there is little else of value in the entire stretch of country thus thrown open). It would free the emigrant route in that direction from the visits of these Indians, unless with license, which is a circumstance strongly favoring this change of the line. Within this broad belt rove the Pah-Utahs, often entering the settlements through the Cajon Pass, to stay awhile feeding on cattle and carry off horses back to their sand-hills. They can be provided for hereafter.

Let this Territory be subdivided into the requisite number of Indian Reserves, distinguished by the names of the nations; the lands to be reserved from sale or private entry, or occupation by others than the Indians, until Congress shall otherwise order, *with their consent.*

If the Federal Government believes that it has the power to legislate with[in] the limits of this State over such a territory and people, let the power be exercised with a firmer hand than it has ever been, and in the full spirit of "the greatest amount of good to the largest number."

The United States District Court ought to be held in the

City of Los Angeles, with a term at San Diego and Santa Barbara; and hence, it may be necessary to make this a separate Judicial District—a measure for which many other sound reasons might be urged, as, for example, its extent and remoteness from San Francisco or Monterey, its rapidly increasing commercial importance, its contiguity to the Mexican territories of Lower California and Sonora, etc.

There will be harpies ever seeking, for a little filthy lucre, to prey upon the body and soul of the Indian, trespass on his lands and fields, cut his timber, create discord and disobedience. Let stringent laws be made for the punishment of trespassers, the sale or introduction of ardent spirits, or trading within said limits—such laws as can be enforced; and, if possible, let the punishments be more summary and prompt than they have been in other territories. These things must be well regulated; and, as it strikes me, agents would have to be invested with considerable discretionary power.

There should be *corporal* punishment for some offences, for instance, selling ardent spirits to Indians within the territory.

Viewing the Indians somewhat in the condition of minors and wards under the guardianship of the Government, we should not rest content with so beautiful a theory, nor treat it as a theory, but act upon it in earnest, even as the parent for his child. I have no sympathy for the white man who would violate a single right of the simple Indian; and the laws should be so framed as to mete out to him, in all such cases, exemplary punishment.

How the Government will be able to adjust the coming "crisis" on the great plains, and reconcile the two extremes of American civilization and Indian barbarism, is a problem that can be solved as well another day. Certain it is, that *here*

the Government has reached the *ultima thule* of political speculation, and something more is necessary—it is a question
that brooks neither weakness nor delay. The Nebraska Territory was a magnificent conception—it may yet be realized.
The principles of eternal justice have barriers for the white
not less than for the red man. A government as just as the
American, should proclaim and sanction them by its policy.
Fortunately for the red man here, nature comes to our help,
in a manner that renders any other policy—impossible!

Not a thousand acres of all the territory proposed are now
occupied by cattle or crops of white men. Only three white
men are actually resident upon any part of it. No great while
ago, it had many a fair garden planted by Indian care—nay,
still has them; and the feet of fifteen thousand of that race
still tread its rocks and leave their traces on its sands.

I have mentioned the "Mexican claims" to portions of it,
as Tejon, San Gorgonio, San Jacinto, Temecula, and Agua
Caliente. If they amount to valid titles, they ought to be respected. I presume that they can be quieted for a reasonable
sum—much more easily than "Indian title" to them can be
"extinguished." But, be the sum largely beyond their real
value to the present claimants, I regard it as of the last importance to the Indians, the Government, and adjoining white
population, to secure these five situations for the permanent
location of the Indians; not a fugitive, equivocal, and uncertain "right of occupancy," but a real and stable property, a
home and homestead forever.

At this moment they may be said truly to be mere wastes,
so far as the hand of man has anything to do with them. The
interests of the claimants appear to direct them elsewhere.
The Indians glean their fruitful surface for a few months' subsistence, but their energy needs to be guided by more enlight-

ened hands than their own. They need the American Government for a little while. All these points once had minor establishments of the missions. They are still the choicest seats of Indian villages.

They are the only places where the different nations could be colonized and established in large numbers, with sufficient land for cultivation. San Gorgonio and San Jacinto each has more than 2,000 acres capable of raising barley and wheat, without irrigation; and sufficient water, husbanded as the Missions taught Indians to manage this matter, to supply in abundance beans, pumpkins, and the other crops Indians are familiar with, or can soon be made so. The beautiful valley of Temecula—the granary of San Luis Rey Mission—presents an agricultural area of three times this capacity; and Agua Caliente and the Tejon are not inferior, perhaps superior to Temecula. In the direction of the Tejon, but rather out of the line proposed, there are other good selections that can be made. The Cahuillas can raise 100,000 bushels of wheat or barley annually, at San Jacinto or San Gorgonio. Temecula and Agua Caliente would yield $300,000 worth of like produce every year for the San Luiseños and Dieguiños. Equal resources would reward the Tulareños at the Tejon. They do not need annuities. Nature has these in ample store, with their mere rights of property secured, and a judicious management. At Agua Caliente, Coyote, and other places, they still have producing vineyards; and at others, orchards; all planted by themselves for the Missions. At Coyote the grape ripens two months sooner than nearer the coast—at Los Angeles, for instance. All these valleys are fine for every species of fruit, as well as for vegetables and small grain. They are well enough timbered for ordinary farming purposes, and as to water, what I have said of San Gorgonio will apply to the rest. There is abundant grass for stock, with wild oats. I have no reason to believe that there is gold or silver in an amount sufficient to justify any of the mining enterprises characteristic of the northern part of the State. There are no other minerals important to be noticed here. The Mohave river offers one other point, in this direction, where a considerable body of Indians might be concentrated and well sustained; and its upper waters might serve for the Cahuillas, in part. The lesser valleys and rivulets might still be made auxiliary to the supply of these people, in like manner as under the Missions—only entrusted to the care of the more trustworthy Indians, and always kept under the commons system. But upon the locations I have attempted to describe should be concentrated and established the mass of the several nations.

THE MILITARY POSTS,

if I may be permitted to make the suggestion which has, probably, been anticipated in the proper quarter, should be at the Four Creeks (or its neighborhood), on the Mohave river, and at the junction of the rivers Gila and Colorado; the first and third, of 100 men each; for the second, a small number would suffice. The distance is about thirty miles to the Mohave from the Cajon Pass, where it enters the valley of San Bernardino. If half a troop of dragoons were stationed here, and half on the Mohave—say, sixty men in all—and a due disposition made respecting the nations now particularly under our notice, the county of Los Angeles would be spared the incursions of Utahs and Pah-Utahs, which have followed every full moon, until within very few months. As many troops are not necessary now as were two and three years ago, because this part of the country is rapidly settling up with a population able, in part, and always willing, to defend themselves. I do not believe that soldiers ought to be kept in the midst of the Indians of whom we are speaking here, save when absolutely necessary to enforce the laws in the extreme cases an Agent might be placed in sometimes. In common practice, he would possess control enough over them, from the fact of his ability to summon troops from a post so near as the Mohave or Cajon Pass, or from a garrison which, I suppose, would always be maintained, of necessity, somewhere in San Diego county—at the rancho of Santa Ysabella, Mission of San Luis Rey, or in the town itself of San Diego. The distance from the Cajon Pass to San Gorgonio is 30 miles; to Temecula, 50 miles, to Agua Caliente, 85 miles. A post on the Mohave river would also serve to take care of the Mohave nation, and watch the passage to the Four Creeks, from the direction of the Great Salt Lake; while that on Porsiuncula river, or the Four Creeks, would fully protect San Luis Obispo, Santa Barbara, and Tulare counties. I may be excused if I add that all the expence of 250 soldiers thus occupied for a couple of years, would not equal the losses which Los Angeles county alone has sustained from Indian depredations in the same length of time—from wild Indians, I mean—to say nothing of the immense losses of the other counties, and of individual travelers and emigrants, besides the sacrifice of numerous valuable lives. Nor should their expences be weighed at all in the balance with the incomparable advantages to be gained and dangers to be avoided by bettering the condition of these Indians whom they would thus protect in the quiet pursuits of industry. If the Indian is to lay down the bow and arrow, he must have some guarantee that it will not be taken up by his natural enemy, and used against him. These troops are an indispensable part of the undertaking we expect to enter into; and a kind and munificent government cannot complain of the comparatively trifling cost of their support on this frontier.

I have said that the Indians can never go back to the Missions; nor is it necessary that they should go back. United States troops are occupying San Diego and San Luis Rey; San Fernando, Santa Barbara, and Santa Ynes are under leases, soon to expire; but it is understood, after a [nominal] two months' notice to the Indians, all of them were sold, somewhere about the end of 1845 and June, 1846. The alleged purchasers, or most of them, are now urging their claims before the Commissioners of Land Titles. There are, also, alleged creditors against the Missions, as against San Gabriel, for example. The rich plains of the one last mentioned, with its vineyards, orchards, and olive groves, are covered with pre-emption claims of white settlers. A fragment of each, with its church, is in possession of a resident priest. I am credibly informed that the Mexican Government remains indebted to the Missions between one and two millions of dollars for supplies furnished the Presidios (garrisons) between 1810 and 1837, the date of their final destruction, in a pecuniary point of view.

If the Indians have a just right to these Missions, or any legal interest in them, it ought to be disposed of, and the proceeds applied to their use; or in such case, if the Missions shall be given up to settlement, like other public land, which seems to be their destiny, situated as they are in the heart of the coast country, an equivalent can be provided for the Indians in the new locations resigned to them by the Government. On the latter supposition, the Government may be more readily reconciled to the cost of quieting claims, removal, establishment, etc.

The value of the Missions, at the date of their secularization in 1834, taking cattle and other personal property into account, could not have been less than (say) $5,000,000. Extend the calculation to land, and it would be almost beyond appreciation. From that date to June (or July), 1846, vineyards, orchards, buildings, all included, they could not have depreciated to less than (say) one million. What a magnificent annuity fund, or capital of bank stock! That so much property should have passed from the hands of the Mission Indians, in the short space of six months, without any known agency of theirs, is an event calculated to leave an impression upon the minds of reflecting men, long after the actors in such a wholesale confiscation shall be forgotten. I well remember the surprise manifested when a knowledge of these sales first became public, which has not subsided to the present day. The proper judicial tribunals will decide upon the question of their legality. What we want for the Indians is a system of measures, immediately to be carried into effect; not the "glorious uncertainties" of a protracted litigation in their behalf, even with the reasonable assurance of gaining them all these splendid structures they have reared, but which in any event, must pass into other hands.[46]

There are many well-meaning men, I know, who favor the idea of restoring them to the Missions; as places wedded to their affections and where they would be more sure to prosper, as in former days. A knowledge of the country forbids the idea: the measure is impracticable. And the sympathy which wastes itself on the impracticable, where the poor Indian is concerned, proves his worst enemy.

[46] Under the operation of the California Land Act of 1851 land titles throughout California were beclouded with uncertainty, glorious or otherwise, and were to continue so for many years. Bancroft, *History of California*, VI, 529-81; Caughey, *California*, 363-78.

I would scarcely discharge my duty to them, if I failed, in this connection, to advert to certain laws which bear strongly on their rights, at least as they strike my humble judgment.

There is a qualified recognition of some of their rights, even by the law of the State of California, passed April 22d, 1850, section second, as follows:

"Persons and proprietors of lands on which Indians are residing, shall permit such Indians peaceably to reside on such lands, unmolested in the pursuit of their usual avocations for the maintenance of themselves and families; provided, the white person, or proprietor, in possession of such lands may apply to a Justice of the Peace in the township where the Indians reside, to set off to such Indians a certain amount of land, and on such application, the Justice of the Peace shall set off a sufficient amount of land for the necessary wants of such Indians, including the site of their village or residence, if they so prefer it; and in no case shall such selection be made to the prejudice of such Indians, nor shall they be forced to abandon their homes or villages where they have resided for a number of years, and either party feeling themselves aggrieved, can appeal to the County Court from the decision of the Justice; and then [when?] divided, a record shall be made of the lands so set off in the court so dividing them, and the Indians shall be permitted to remain thereon until otherwise provided for."

No such division of lands has been made among the Indians—at least, to my knowledge. The practical efficacy of the State law may be judged of from the fact that the Indians I am speaking of "reside" in a "township" equal to Rhode Island and Delaware put together, without a Justice of the Peace nearer than thirty miles, in general, nor likely to be nearer within the next hundred years. And what do they or can they know of "appeals" and County Courts? Or, if they did know, who would plead their cause?

On the same day, a law was passed repealing "all laws now in force in this State, except such as have been passed or adopted by Legislature," but without affecting any "rights acquired, contracts made, or suits pending, nor any constitutional laws or acts of Congress, or any of the stipulations contained in the treaty of peace between the United States and Mexico, ratified at Queretaro, the 30th of May, 1848."

It was a generous provision of the Spanish law which declared: "After distributing among the Indians whatever they may justly want to cultivate, sow, and raise cattle, confirming to them what they now hold, and granting what they may want besides, all the remaining land may be reserved to us [the King], clear of any incumbrance, for the purpose of being given as rewards, or disposed of according to our pleasure." (White's Land Laws, vol. 2, p. 52.) Lands could never be granted, without notice to the Indians. (Ib., p. 95.) The old permits of settlement to retired soldiers in California will be found with the clause, "without prejudice to the Indians." Nor could the subjected Indians be deprived of their lands, as the law declares: "Whereas, the Indians would sooner and more willingly be reduced into settlements, if they were allowed to retain the lands and improvements which they possess in the districts from which they shall remove; we command that no alteration be made therein, and that the same be left to them, to be owned as before, in order that they may continue to cultivate them and dispose of their produce" (Ib., p. 59).

There can be no doubt, then, that under the Spanish laws, these Indians of whom we treat have a right to their villages and pasture lands, to the extent of their wants, "as their common property, by a perpetual right of possession;" in the words of the Supreme Court of the United States, "a possession considered with reference to Indian habits and modes of life; and the hunting grounds of the tribes were as much in their actual occupation as the cleared fields of the whites." (9 Peters' U. S. Reports, p. 711.) Theirs, indeed, is the only real occupation or cultivation all those fine tracts we have spoken of ever had; and the whole will be just "sufficient for the necessary wants of such Indians," in the language of the State law, whose spirit only imitates the beneficient principles which pervaded all the laws of the Indies, where this unhappy race were concerned.

Turn again to the Missions.

No past mal-administration of those laws can be suffered to destroy their true intent, while the victims of mal-administration live to complain, and all the rewards of wrong have not been consumed. Of all that noble estate earned by the Indians through half a century of toil, a little is left. 'Tis not now "natural rights" I speak of, nor merely possessory, but "rights acquired and contracts made," to quote the State law again—acquired and made when the laws of the Indies had force here, never assailed by any laws or executive acts till 1834 or 1846, (and impregnable to all these,) shielded not only by the laws of California, but, before, by the Constitution of the United States, and which, in virtue of the treaty of peace, can safely be entrusted to the justice and wisdom of the Federal Judiciary.

If the Fathers were ever more, in the laws, than trustees or guardians of their neophytes, I am unable to see it. If the neophytes ever had other legal relation to them than of wards, it must have been of slaves. A certain oblique or inconsiderate way of viewing history, might lead some persons hastily to such a supposition. Admit the *fact* of slavery, if you please; no idea, in respect to the neophytes, would be more abhorrent to the *law*. The Indians of California never were slaves, by virtue of any law. Let the laws and their connection with the Missions speak for them, in as brief a recapitulation as I can possibly embrace the opinions which I wish to convey.

Their right of occupancy does not date back only eighty-two years ago, to the appearance of the Fathers among them —an event which their old men and women still describe in their own simple style."When the Indians come to us," says the founder of all these Missions,"we give them food and clothing; so, soon we shall gain their confidence, and be able to teach them to discern good from evil." When the Fathers and the soldiers failed of supplies and nearly famished, the Indians gathered the wild seeds to feed them.When the former became stronger and more numerous, the neophytes supported them from the mission produce. And, from the beginning to the end, the Indians paid all the expenses of the government. Under the laws of the Indies, they adopted the discipline of the Fathers, and nearly all were subjugated to the faith. At any rate, so the all-confident Fathers proclaimed it, and we cannot doubt their sincerity, even if we may their judgment. The Indians became "reduced," in the expressive language of the laws.

Can we believe that, through all, day and night, and in every lesson, the natives did not hear of those laws made by the good and kind Spanish monarchs? No! The Fathers must have preached them as often as any other truth, to inspire their disciples with a hope equal to their constant labor.Their submission was the result of many things combined, but I seem to see in it inducements and promises—considerations, would not be an unapt expression—such as never have existed between American rulers and an Indian tribe. Call it—law! Call it—force! These were its sanctions, instruments of its execution. But the whole wears more the aspect of solemn treaty—rather an almost infinite series of treaties—binding forever the faith of the Spanish crown, and not less its republican successors.

Religion, "pure and undefiled," would seem to have been its basis. If we may credit the laws and instructions, certain actual benefits and the substantial blessings temporal which all covet were to be the price—and who will say they could be an equivalent?—of the life of toil to which the savages bound themselves and posterity. There is but one impulse of human nature capable of sustaining them: self-interest! And how hopefully each generation must have struggled on in that weary race! Not *all* "a spiritual conquest," "a civilized and rational life!"—but "mission pueblos," "to become cities, and houses of adobe or of stone and morter"—"a garden, where the Indian shall sow some seeds and herbs and plant trees"— "thus holding them with constancy to the place." More than all the rest: "common lands" and "individual concessions to such Indians as may most dedicate themselves to agriculture and the raising of cattle: for," continue these instructions, August 17, 1773, to the commandant of San Diego and Monterey, "having property of their own, the love of it will cause them to plant themselves more firmly." Fond illusion! Tribe after tribe it drew to the sacred portals. Carried down through a weary length of years! To this hour cherished by many a dark-skinned child of the mountains! Never, perchance, inscribed on parchment—yet written indelibly upon the Indian's heart!

Never was a more solemn treaty ratified before heaven. Never before, or since, was a contract so shamelessly violated.

Long ago the Indians did their part to fulfil it. The venerable Fathers left no stain upon their good faith. To have snatched away the cup brimful for fruition, is the reproach of other men, whose acts—as the wrong is not yet *all* consummated— will be judged by a Government from which "vested rights" will receive due protection.

No unbending prescription has hallowed the wrong. The true history of the Missions, when it shall be written, will not authorize the assertion that the Indians "abandoned" them, and so incurred a forfeiture of their legal rights, or placed themselves out of the power of the authorities to comply with their duties under the laws. The authorities—God knows!— always had power enough; and the world knows it. Here, at least, these Indians have "property," as well as "occupancy."

From the first, portions of the natives repulsed the kind approaches of the Fathers, it is true. They clung tenaciously to their mountain villages. There, reunited at length with neophytes and their descendants, they maintain an organized existence as political societies—of an inferior grade, indeed, but quite as distinct and substantial as is observable in many other tribes under the jurisdiction of the United States. Do what he may, and wander where he will for a time, there is no other resting-place at last for the neophyte but at the fires of his tribe. This state of things impartial history will attribute to the secularization of the Missions, in the manner it was effected, and the multitude of irregular and illegal acts consequent upon that unfortunate measure. For none can doubt that then the Indians were ripe for the last achievements in that experiment of which they had borne the burden so many years. Common tradition, even now, whether among Indians or whites, tells of the beauty, order, and comfort with which everything went on at a Mission: the charming simplicity and decorum of the Indians; their industry, honesty, and intelligence. It was a Manchester or Lowell, on a small scale. It may be, the Fathers became too fond of the pleasures and importance which wealth and power bring with them. They gave no signs of corruption, however, in their dealings with their people. They must have had too little confidence in the white community around them; and, perchance, foresaw the storm ahead, and fancied they alone could brave and shield their "little ones" from its rage. To me it seems, had they put on at once the energy of the Jesuits, and, like those valiant priests in Lower California, resisting power and avarice with an iron front, moulded their little communities to the shape which the ancient laws designed, all would have been saved. They might have done this in 1830, or before. The blow once struck, they had ample time to repent their weakness; and all who succeeded them, to deplore its consequences.[47]

I have treated their rights with candor, if not well. Less I could not have said in justice to myself, as a representative of their interests, which appeal so strongly to the attention of the Government.

I now proceed to offer some recommendations for their management.

MANAGEMENT.

Upon the whole, I wish to see preserved the principal machinery which has been adopted for the government of the other more advanced tribes. A sub-agent, farmer, blacksmith, and carpenter would be necessary for each town, there being eight towns in all, with those of the Mojaves and Yumas; an inter-

[47] There are less glowing descriptions of life at the missions; for example, in Bancroft's and Chapman's histories of California and in Carey McWilliams, *Southern California Country* (New York, 1946).

preter and teacher, likewise, for each town. The duties of such officers are well specified in the existing regulations, it being understood that some of these regulations do not apply here, (and such can be readily distinguished).

Would it not be better to commence teaching with the Spanish language, under the present circumstances? I incline to think it would, but possibly not, as they are to be reared to the uses of American civilization, with which its language is closely identified. They have a great capacity for learning languages—perhaps I have mentioned this before.

For teachers, at first, and for a long time, we should have to depend on the religious or benevolent societies: this would be the best, if they can be induced to embark promptly in this great task.

Their religious affairs, of course, should be left to the different Christian denominations, showing equal favor to all.

Good farmers and interpreters, as well as many minor officials requisite for these nations, can be found here in each of the nations, or among those of Indian descent.

Sub-agents and master carpenters and blacksmiths, and, indeed, all persons employed among the nations, should be men of families; this ought to be almost a *sine qua non*. Salaries would be raised proportionately.

The schools should be conducted on some uniform plan, in its main features to be regulated by law. Religion, I hope, will not be without its faithful ministers; but, to avoid all difficulties ensuing upon a possible difference of theological tenets, the schools should be confined to studies not of a sectarian character. Every other facility ought to be extended to the ministers of the gospel, in their efforts for the regeneration of this race. It is a fine field for their labors. If I do not completely mistake the character of these Indians, they will yield themselves to instruction more readily than almost any other tribe in the Union. Experience, however, satisfies me that the schools ought to be regulated by law, and not the discretion of each society—some simple and practical law. Attendance on school certain hours and days in the week, the kinds of punishments or rewards, branches to be taught, etc., might be subjects of regulation. Parents should be compelled to send their children to school, under some penalty; this there may seldom be occasion to inflict.

Manual labor schools, perhaps, are desirable; but of this I am not certain. Boys will be withdrawn from school very often, to assist their parents on the farm, in the garden or workshop—those of the larger size, particularly. Labor and study will thus conflict even more than is advisable. Rather let them be pushed on with their studies for a year or two.

There are *Indian women* capable of teaching the girls plain needlework, washing and ironing, and a various household knowledge. These should be kept in employ on salaries, a few in each town. This will encourage them, and they may be among the most efficient civilizers.

Their common government, religion, and education being disposed of, let us observe rather more in detail the other necessary points in their management.

They ought to be required absolutely to reside on their respective territories or reserves, and not to leave unless with license from the sub-agents, upon reasons fixed by law, or in cases of necessity, to be judged of by the sub-agents. Any laws intended for their benefit must keep in view to some extent, the character and wants of the neighboring white population. Some of these Indians would, probably, still wish to bind themselves as servants in families, as before; they ought to be permitted to leave the Territory for this purpose; why might not the contract of hiring be required to be made before the sub-agent, not to exceed a year without renewal? "Madrinas," (Godmothers), here agreeably to Spanish usage, have a great taste for keeping Indian children till they become of age or marry; there are many orphans whom their parents have left to the possession and care of particular friends, and others for whom the Probate Court has appointed guardians (so-called). Others would hang about the towns as vagabonds, and ought to be removed to a place where they can be controlled, and have motives to be better. Fugitives from the State laws would fly to the Territory, and *vice versa*. White men would hover on the border of the Territory, to trade with Indians, etc. A *State law* should prohibit, like that of Missouri, all trading with Indians, *in the counties here mentioned*, and outside of the Territory or Reserves, for provisions, clothing, horses, cattle, indeed any personal property—at least there should be a temporary law of this trade. A good State law would be necessary for many other purposes connected with this plan; the present State law is clearly inadequate to the exigencies of these Indians.

PRESENT STATE LAW.

We may fairly presume that the State law now in force was not intended to be permanent. In addition to the provision above quoted touching lands, it extends the civil and criminal laws of the State over all Indians within its limits; prohibits their punishment, except by justices of the peace, with a jury (if required); subjects them to fine or whipping, not to exceed 25 lashes for stealing; gives the Indians power to require the chiefs and influential men of any village to apprehend, and bring before the justices any Indian charged or suspected of an offence; and "if any tribe or village refuse or neglect to obey the laws, the justice of the peace may punish the guilty chiefs or principle men by reprimand or fine, or otherwise reasonably chastise them." If convicted, Indians may be hired out to pay the fine and costs for a time fixed by the justice. A white man is finable for "abducting an Indian from his home, or compelling him to work against his will," and for selling or giving him intoxicating liquors (except in sickness)—and, for the last offence may be imprisoned not less than five days. Contracts for hiring must be in writing made before a justice of the peace. In like manner a minor Indian child may be bound out by parents or friends till the age of 18, if a male, and a female till 15, these being their ages of majority. For vagrancy—"loitering and strolling about, or frequenting public places where liquors are sold, begging, or leading an immoral or profligate course of life," he is hired out at public auction, a term not longer than four months, to be subject to the law regulating guardians and minors, unless he can give bail for good behavior for twelve months; the proceeds of his hire, after deducting certain expenses, to be paid to his family, if he have one, if not, like fines to be paid into the county treasury. The only additional remedial provision is one making it "the duty of justices of the peace, in their respective townships, as well as all other peace officers in this State, to instruct the Indians in their neighborhood in the laws which relate to them, giving them such advice as they may deem necessary!"

All punishment. *No* reform!

TOWNS.

There ought to be at least one principal town, or *pueblo* on each of the reserves. I think, however, that the Tulareños and Cahuillas might manage their resources to better advantage, each being divided into towns. In round numbers, then, those that can be immediately provided for may be distributed as follows: 1st, Four Creeks, (Tulareños,) 1,000; 2d. Tejon, (same,) 1,000; 3d, San Gorgonio, (Cahuillas,) 1,500; 4th, San Jacinto, (same,) 1,500; 5th, Temecula, (San Luiseños,) 1,000; 6th, Agua Caliente, (Dieguiños) 1,000; 7th, Mouth of Gila, (Yumas,) 1,000; 8th, Upper Colorado, (Mohaves,) 1,000. For the present the two last may be excluded from view, as they require some peculiar arrangements in their behalf. The distance from one town to another is as follows, viz: From Four Creeks to Tejon, say 100 miles; thence to San Gorgonio, 130; thence to San Jacinto, say 12; thence to Temecula, say 15; thence to Agua Caliente, 35 miles; that is by the usual routes.

The body of the people should have their houses and residences in the towns. The sites of these and the manner of building them are matters which a people can determine after they become settled, have raised a crop, and have time to look about them. They should be built as compactly as health will admit of, and let the "laws of the Indies," and some other Spanish laws, suggest a part of the regulations, if better ones cannot be devised in these days of progress. For the present, the rude architecture of the Indians would answer. Let us "hasten slowly" in some things.

IMMEDIATE SUPPORT.

One thousand head of cattle, with their own natural resources, would amply support them for six months. These can be delivered and slaughtered at the sites mentioned for $30,000. They would need, also, at the beginning, a small supply of common clothing—blankets, hats, calico, and brown cotton sheeting; farming and mechanical implements, and some

work animals, mules or oxen. A physician and some medi-
cines are among the earliest requisites towards a moral reform,
which must not forget the physical. First and last, they would
be taught that on their own physical exertions they must rely
for subsistence, and that all these measures were only designed as a helping hand towards that end. Afterwards, they
could not only support themselves, but defray all the expenses
of their officers, if proper to do so. They have done more than
this before, and can do it again. The Missions, doubtless,
taught this lesson, from father to son. Stern necessity has since
indelibly impressed it upon their minds. They will not be apt
to retain false ideas on the subject of self-dependence.

COMMON LANDS.

The land of each Town should be held common until such
time as it may be deemed expedient to dispose of it otherwise,
and should be cultivated by the whole of the people who are
not assigned to other pursuits.

There should be hours of labor, rest, and amusement, not
entirely losing sight of their olden-time sports, and new ones
may be invented.

The division of labor among the different classes, planting,
sowing, irrigation and cultivation, harvest, building, fencing,
care of stock, and various other things of their economy, can
only be judged of by competent men on the spot. They should
be left to the rules which a discreet agent may frame under
the approbation of the proper department.

It will not excite surprise that such a proposition should
be made, when known that within 30 miles of one of these
proposed communities, a settlement of 500 Mormons hold
their land in community, build splendid mills, cut long roads
up steep mountains, cultivate common wheat fields of 2,000

acres enclosed, by the joint labor of the whole people, and enjoy harmony, content, and prosperity withal.[48] Good neighbors to the Indians, and a model for them! With few exceptions, the Mormons are congregated in a small town, built a year or so ago, for defence against some of the same Indians. In another year, perhaps, agreeably to American usage and necessity, the former will each live upon his separate farm, and till it according to his taste or sense of his interests. But, would this policy be advisable for the Indians—at this time? For the great mass of them it would not, I think.

INDIVIDUAL CONCESSIONS.

There are many objections to allowing them to live dispersed, in this, their first stage of improvement. It interferes too much with education, and deprives them measurably of instruction in religion; takes them from under the eye of their officers and influence of good examples, exposes them to the practices of evil-disposed persons who may be lurking about the territory, and otherwise puts them in the way of temptation, and tends to weaken the tie of a common *public interest* which requires to be sustained by more than ordinary means where different villages are thus to be amalgamated, as it were, under a common system.

Moreover, the locations here suggested for them, are not suitable for their dispersion in small farms, to any great number—nor do I believe that the Missions were, in general. They would be sufficient for men content to be half-starved through the year. Their full resources could not thus be developed. San Gorgonio, for example, would not support a hundred small farmers, seeking to satisfy the wants of civilization; while, under a common cultivation, and a systematic

[48] The reference, of course, is to San Bernardino.

and economical appropriation of the water for irrigation, it will amply support three thousand souls, and more.[49]

The few "land proprietors," and the overseers and hands of the minor establishments would not be excepted from this rule, though the former would consent to remove to the reserves, on no other condition, probably; and might be permitted at once to own small separate tracts. But, it would be better to make a different arrangement with them; the superior skill they have in agriculture qualifies them to be the instructors and managers of the rest, in various employments that might be found for them. There is a very common practice here, of farming, even with Americans, who wish to save fencing, for instance, that suggests equitable provisions among the Indians by which a species of separate property may be preserved, with common fields, zanjas, &c. With, or without, separate farms, they should long be required to have their habitations within the town limits—a necessary requirement for police purposes.

In the course of time "individual concessions" might be made to such Indians as "may most dedicate themselves to agriculture and the raising of cattle," being just rewards of their proficiency, and strong incentives to emulation among the rest, and consequent improvement. They are not ready for this measure now.

COMMON STOCK—COMPULSORY LABOR.

I am not sure that I can recommend *a restraint* to be put upon them, different in principle from that which has been exercised towards other tribes of the United States, in remarkable cases. If mine would be greater in degree, it is the result of

[49] This is cogent appraisal of the problems of efficient land utilization in the southern California environment.

my observation of the character of these particular nations, and the circumstances that surround them. They require a vigilance, as much for their own protection as to prevent them from doing wrong to the other inhabitants. And the country they would live in, and the climate, at once inculcate and favor their concentration in large bodies, not less than the necessity they will feel to have a fixed and watchful government.

Their wastefulness furnishes a sufficient reason for requiring most of their productions—all their wheat and corn, for instance, to be kept in a common stock, and to be dealt out to them by certain rules, in daily, or tri-weekly rations. Otherwise, no amount of provisions would last them through the year, until by long habit they shall have reformed in this respect.

An immemorial law of the Pimos, and one secret of their success in agriculture beyond their neighbors, compels every able-bodied man to work a certain number of days in the week. No better regulation could be devised for these nations, fixing also, a limited number of working hours every day (except Sunday). It is the same they were accustomed to under the Missions. In some civilized agricultural and mechanical districts, custom and the exactions of capital, fix this matter with an oppression much more severe on the individual man, than can be felt by these Indians, under their genial sun, and on a soil yielding as much as most other countries, with half the labor. Let it be the "*six*-hour system!" if you will.

These two rules—a common-stock and compulsory labor—are absolutely indispensable to their welfare, at the incipiency of any plan. Thus far, the Government would lead them back to the Mission system. All the balance will tend to reform and mould it to suit our own institutions.

CODE OF LAWS.

Such communities as are here proposed to be created—or rather, re-organized—will need a plain and simple code of laws and "ordinances" adapted to their genius and pursuits, to be changed according to the state of their progress. Unlike the wild tribes, they are prepared for this step. They have a very correct notion of right and wrong; value life and property; are familiar with the idea of "alcalde" (Magistrate); like speedy accusation and trial; are used to obedience.

They are easily governed. Fines may do for some—*corporal* punishment will be best to restrain others; it may be tolerated for a year or two yet, in California, "at the discretion of the Court;" nor should rewards be forgotten.

Their local code, whatever it may be, ought to be administered by officers, either Indians or of Indian descent, as far as possible. I am not prepared to say that they can safely be their own legislators, for the first year or two. I do not believe they would desire to be; but, on the contrary, would be glad to adopt in all things the advice of the Government.

Stealing and personal trespasses would be the offences commonly committed; these should be punished on the spot, their chiefs being the "justices of the peace," (for the present), with appeal to the sub-agent; nor would it be inadvisable to accustom them to trial by jury. Murder would be tried and punished differently. The agent and sub-agents must have the power, in some cases, to punish summarily as for disobedience of their lawful orders. One guard against the abuse of power would be, to require a report of all such cases, under oath, to the proper department.

In questions of property between them, the sub-agent may constitute a tribunal, of the nature of courts of conciliation in Mexico, formerly in use here, and very well adapted to the understanding of these Indians, as they were to that of the common run of "whites," six years ago, whose most important disputes were settled often in this way. The appeal from such a court consists simply in the declaration, "I do not agree;" in such case, it being the duty of the sub-agent to transfer the cause to the agent, when the amount should exceed (say) $20; provided that sub-agents, or agents should report to the proper department, briefly, the facts of all such cases; as well as a short statement of all criminal cases disposed of. Such a report might be made to the district attorney of the United States.

It is not important to retain the present distinctions of chiefs. The desire of power and place may be as well gratified by the substitution of other analagous offers of more civilized life, such as justices of the peace and sheriff. These appointments should emanate from the superintendent or agent, and depend upon good behavior. They are accustomed to this mode of filling even the office of chief, and sometimes pride themselves on it, as an evidence of their standing with the whites. Gen. Kearney appointed Antonio Garra to be chief, and "breveted" Juan Antonio a "general;" and the Mexican authorities did so as a regular practice.

These Indians can be trained to self-government in a short time; still, the elective franchise is not the most material thing, just now, for their happiness. But, let them be governed with the least possible violence to their personal independence and freedom; and so that, in all measures, they may be able to discover the strict justice of the government.

Such is a rude sketch of a plan which, I believe, would promote the happiness of the Mission Indians, and which, or something tending to that end, I fervently hope, may be soon matured and finally established by the wisdom of our lawgivers. If duly weighed, the more serious objections to it will be found to have been answered, at one place or another, in the course of the foregoing remarks; and where such objections have not been met directly, and in [explicit] terms, or if new ones may suggest themselves to a cautious reader, all the facts necessary for the solution of his doubts, I trust, may have been sufficiently laid before him.

One word I will add: Considered in their relation to agriculture, in this part of California, these Indians are the only farmers living here, besides the Americans who have come into the country since the war, and a very few who were here before. The California "Spaniard," (so to speak) loves his fiery steed—not the plough. Many such a *ranchero*, rich in cattle and "goodly acres," by the ten thousand, must go to his Indian neighbor hard by on the rancho, if he would dine today on his maize or *frijole!* This remark is made, subject only to isolated exceptions, and as authorizing a general inference much more favorable to the Indian than my incidental description of him, merely as a farm-laborer; for, in a multitude of instances on the numerous ranchos, even where he neither owns land, nor claims more than a casual occupancy, he is more than a *peon* (servant). A very independent and useful producer is the Mission Indian, in such case, whose house and furniture need no insurance, but without whom a *rancho* would eat much less bread and vegetables! That agriculture must be at a low ebb, under such circumstances, may well be inferred. For all that, let us organize, cherish, and improve it, even in the hardy hands we find it, restoring to them their just rights, wherein rejoicing they may push on to the bright goal which American civilization points out to them.

YUMAS.

The Yumas range from New river to the Colorado, and through the country between the latter river and the Gila, but, may be said to inhabit the bottom lands of the Colorado, near the junction of the Gila and the Colorado. Here the first missionaries found them about the year 1776-7, and made two establishments which were soon destroyed. They were formed on a plan different from the Missions above spoken of,[50] in this, that the Fathers cared only for spiritual matters, leaving the Indians, after they were baptized, to live in their *rancherias* and support themselves as before, among the unconverted. Eight soldiers, and as many settlers with their families, formed *pueblos*. "As the Fathers had no presents to make to them," says the old narrative,[51] "the reduction of the Indians was difficult; still they frequented the pueblos to traffic with the soldiers and settlers. Through this intercourse and the aid of a good interpreter, the Fathers succeeded in baptising a few; and, as these did not live in the pueblos, but in their rancherias with the Gentiles, having the same freedom and customs, they very seldom came near the Mission to say their prayers. The Fathers were thus under the necessity of hunting them up through the rancherias and staying some days with them to say the catechism, teach them a little, and attract them to mass on holy days, all of which gave much labor and molestation to the Fathers. Add to this, the resentment of the Gentiles at seeing the grass and other herbage consumed by the horses and cattle of the soldiers and settlers, so that they were deprived of the seeds which before sup-

[50] This experimental deviation from the regular mission system is described in Charles E. Chapman, *A History of California, The Spanish Period* (New York, 1921), 330-42.
[51] Palou, *Relación histórica*.

ported most of them. They saw at the same time that the settlers had appropriated the small parcel of available land, and that they could no longer sow there, as before, their corn, beans, squashes, and water-melons."

If the Fathers did little for the Indians, they seem to have been successful with the soldiers and settlers, for, continues the narrative, "fearfull of some ill to happen from such Indians in the manner they talked, the Fathers applied themselves to keep the settlers and soldiers prepared for death * * so that they seemed more like monasteries than pueblos." One Sunday just after the last mass, an immense number of Indians fell upon both settlements at the same moment, and but one man escaped death or captivity. Not a great while afterwards the captives were delivered up to an expedition sent against the Indians. I should not omit the beautiful vision of angels clad in white robes, with burning torches and chanting an unknown tongue and strain, that, according to the history, for many nights after moved in procession round and round the scene of martyrdom, giving joy to the captives, but striking such terror into the minds of the Indians, that they abandoned their lands and fled some eight leagues down the river!

This tragedy put a stop to the design which had been formed of establishing the new missions of California upon the plan of those on the Colorado. Two of the existing missions of Santa Barbara county were immediately afterwards founded, with the happy results we have seen upon the Indians.

The recent military operations against the Yumas[52] have doubtless made the Government fully acquainted with their character, customs and resources; though, it must be confessed, a state of war does not afford the best opportunity to

[52] The Morehead expedition; see p. xxiii.

judge national character, whether Indian or civilized. In respect to the Indian, too, we are very apt to overlook the causes which drive him to war. Had the Yumas received no provocation in the spring and summer of 1850 from reckless white men—I allude to the circumstances attending the death of John Glanton—there is little probability that the heavy expenses of those military operations would have been incurred. The State expedition that followed the massacre of Glanton's party, however well meant, made none but the most unfavorable impression upon them, in respect to the American character for bravery or our national power. Let it be considered, also, that they have no doubt been greatly vitiated, and misled in relation to Americans, by the corrupt and worthless set of Sonoranians who have been passing through their country, within the last four years to and from the gold mines of California. Under proper management, I believe, the Yumas will be found nearly, if not quite as tractable as the nations already spoken of. To think of a Yuma in the light of a Sioux, or Camanche, where war is concerned, would be one of the strongest contrasts that could be presented. Now, when at last they have come to know the power of our Government, they are better prepared to receive the next and best manifestation of its virtues, in some efficient plan for their improvement.

The Yumas are large, well-formed, sprightly, and intelligent in their appearance; are inveterate gamblers, like most of these Indians; still tolerate polygamy, but their women have a reputation for chastity. A climate of perpetual summer does not call for much clothing; and, as there is very little rain, a house of brush thrown over a few poles answers every want. What was true of their agriculture in 1776 is still true, except that they have added wheat to their products. "They depend in a great measure upon the cultivation of the soil, for their support," says Russell Sackett, Esq., who spent a considerable time among them, "and although their cultivation is of the rudest kind, receiving little or no attention after the planting, yet their crops mature with an astonishing growth. Their planting season is usually in the month of July, after the waters of the Colorado begin to fall. They then seek those portions of the bottom lands that have been overflowed during the high water, and put in the crop. These lands retain the moisture after having been once flooded, a sufficient length of time to produce a crop without any further irrigation. The crops cultivated principally are corn, beans, peas, squashes, and melons, all of which they raise with very little labor. Wheat also does well there. It was put in about the first of January, and ripened about the first of June."

The distance from Los Angeles city to the mouth of the Gila is 280 miles; from San Diego about 2— miles, and somewhat less by the more southern route. The Colorado river is navigable by steamboats from the gulf to the mouth of the Gila, and in the season of high water, which is from May to September, a boat drawing eight feet of water would usually find no difficulty in ascending far above the mouth of the Gila; and the Gila itself, at some seasons can be ascended by steamboats of light draught, such as are seen on the Ohio and Missouri waters, even to the villages of the Pimos (a distance of 190 miles by land from the mouth of the Gila.) A further quotation from Mr. Sackett is worth[y] of attention, and reliable:

"The soil of the bottom lands along the Colorado and Gila rivers is exceedingly rich, and the climate in that section of the country is not surpassed in its salubrity by any in the world.* * Above the confluence of the Colorado and the Gila, the former river runs for some distance very nearly south. At this confluence it makes an angle and runs thence for a few miles, due west. The tract of land lying within this angle, commencing fifteen or twenty miles below, reaching from the river back to the mountains, contains an area of thirty or forty square miles, and is all susceptible of cultivation. But, in order to cultivate to any great extent, the land must be irrigated, and that will be attended with considerable expense, as the water must be taken out several miles above to get it on these bottom lands, as for damming the Colorado, I hold that it is impracticable. The tract of country lying between the Colorado and Gila is also excellent land, and may be as easily cultivated and irrigated as that lying west of the Colorado. The timber along the river, although abundant, is of poor quality, being none other than the cottonwood, willow and mezquit."

All observers concur in opinion, that the soil and climate are admirably fitted to the cultivation of cotton, rice, sugar, sweet potatoes, and nearly all the tropical fruits. They possess natural resources of fruit, fish, and aquatic fowl, more abundantly than any of the other nations here spoken of, in addition to a soil capable of yielding them all necessaries of life, under the most indolent cultivation. With an active industry inspired by the paternal counsels, and guided by the hand of an enlightened government, they may be able at no distant day, to raise themselves to a comfortable independence, if not to a high degree of prosperity and wealth. In their vicinity they have a striking example for their own emulation, and not less to encourage our government, in the quiet, industrious and comparatively happy condition of the Pimos of Sonora.

I have already stated that their language is the same as that of the Dieguiños; and, all other things considered, it does seem to me that Yuma and Dieguiño are not so foreign in nature and habits, as to forbid the application of the same system of civilization to both of them.

The settlement of American citizens on the Colorado, in sufficient number to interfere seriously with the operations of such a system, is too remote a contingency for present consideration.

The Yumas may number 3,000 souls.

The Mohaves, of an equal number, (conjecturally), occupy the country north of the Yumas, and east and south-east of the Cahuillas. All the information we have of them leads me to believe that they would be more easily managed than even the Yumas. Their habits and natural resources for subsistence, are pretty much the same as those of the Cahuillas in the mountain villages; except that they cultivate the land to a greater extent, raising much wheat.

A formal visit to those nations would be very useful towards perfecting a plan for Congress at once to make a small appropriation for defraying the necessary expenses of presents, etc.

A word or two in conclusion.

Nowhere else in the United States is there a people once more than half-civilized that betray such signs of retrogradation as do most of those we have been contemplating. With the aborigines whom the vivifying principles of American civilization thus far have touched at all, the word is onward! Knowledge is perceptibly on the increase among them, if they know less than the Californian. It is always improvement, even if they gain a little skill in the arts each year, beyond the acquirements of the proceeding one, and that skill yet inferior to the Californians'. But *here* we have the other side of the Indian portraiture: To say the least, all is stationary. The worst is a palpable tendency to utter demoralization and ruin.

None will say that they do not deserve a better fate. None here but see and lament their sad condition, and feel the urgent necessity for an immediate change.

The question is, *what shall be the remedy?*

For, longer delay clearly would not be just nor reasonable, nor consistent with any of the maxims which have heretofore guided the American government in its conduct towards the Indians.

There were not wanting patriots who deplored and condemned the secularization of the Missions, at the time and in the manner it took place. Others would have retrieved its disastrous sequel of malversion and destruction, if the power had rested in their hands. Let the innumerable petty revolutions of those days account for a part of the wrong suffered to be done to a people then undoubtedly semi-civilized. Charity may throw her veil over all the rest—all, I mean, that lies beyond the reach of remedial justice.

At the close of the late war, a thousand extraordinary causes disarmed the energy of the Federal Government, so that only now it begins to be felt in California.

It is not strange that the State government, driven in its infancy to expenditures on the scale of an old empire almost, and busy the three years past with the perplexed affairs of its white population—and having very narrow sources of revenue withal—should not have impressed the salutary influences of a wise legislation upon the southern Indians, at a distance of six hundred miles from its capital, whose members were unknown and character completely misconceived. Nor can it be imagined that the people of this State have ever desired, or will desire to put upon its treasury the burden of governing these Indians, and a hundred thousand more within its borders.

Still less will they covet the greater burden and cost of an attempt to exterminate such a multitude of tribes, many of them savage and warlike, whose means and mode of life, though very meagre and very miserable, enable them to sustain an almost endless resistance. After all, the experiment of extermination inevitably resolves itself into the better one of preservation and government, and, having wasted much blood and treasure, we are compelled to do at last, what it were always more discreet, as well as more humane and just, to do at the beginning.

An illustration occurs to me not without its lesson. Two little expeditions made in the South since the spring of 1850 —one against the Yumas, the other against Antonio Garra— cost the people of California at least $150,000. Will any one believe that their results have been commensurate with what the same sum would have effected, if differently applied among the same southern Indians? I have no hesitation in saying that such a sum would have put in operation and maintained three years, on the plan above proposed, the whole six Indian towns, and left them now flourishing and far on the road of progress!

Humanity, not war is the true policy for them. This is the voice of all experience.

The hardships of their case may well claim the cooperation of the State authorities in the manner already indicated, but can only be provided for fully out of the munificence of the Union.

Five years more of indifference on the part of the Federal Government, added to the eighteen of neglect and injury now endured, is more than enough to fill up the cup of misery and complete their destruction. Happily, the Government has not so much to contend with, as it had a short time since.

Soldiers adhere to their duty. The extravagance of the "gold mania" is fast disappearing, and more rational ideas of the price of labor prevail. Good men will serve for fairer salaries. The Indians themselves, and their country are well understood. There are, or ought to be, no "over-ruling circumstances" now to counteract the benign designs of the Government.

Meanwhile, the temper of the American people displays no less the warm benevolence that has kindled up so many enterprises in behalf of this race, and, I firmly believe, will be loth to confess itself unequal to the task which, under Spanish auspices, came so near glorious accomplishment.

I have the honor to be your obedient servant.

CONTEMPORARY COMMENT

THE FIRST *impulse was to arrange the following statements under such headings as "The Indians of Los Angeles and vicinity," "Marauders from the desert," "Wilson and his report," and "Beale and the reservation at Tejon." In real life these various aspects were not so neatly packaged, but were interrelated and intermingled, as they are, for that matter, in several of the individual comments. It seemed wiser, therefore, to use a chronological arrangement, through which, it is hoped, the several topical factors can still be discerned.*

*

REDICK McKEE, GEORGE W. BARBOUR, AND
OLIVER M. WOZENCRAFT, *Indian Commissioners for California,*
TO LUKE LEA, *Commissioner of Indian Affairs*

Camp Barlow, California, May 15, 1851

... The Indians we have met here are generally a hale, healthy, good looking people, not inferior to their red brethren in the southwestern States; and, from having among them many who in early life were attached to the old missions of this country, have already some knowledge of letters, of stock-raising, and agriculture. We think they will, therefore, make rapid improvement when schools, &c., shall be established among them.

We have found by experience that the best way to keep these Indians of California quiet and peaceable is to give them plenty of food. With beef occasionally, and a little flour to mix with the pulverized acorn, making their favorite *panoli,* nothing can induce them to quarrel with the whites....

[*Report of the Commissioner of Indian Affairs,* 1851, p. 485.]

71

GEORGE W. BARBOUR TO LUKE LEA

San Francisco, July 28, 1851

... Immediately after concluding the treaty on King's river I despatched runners to the tribes north of Kearn river, desiring them to meet me on the Cahwia river, at a place designated, some thirty-five or forty miles distant from our camp on King's river. As soon as provisions arrived from Stockton (distant about one hundred and eighty miles) for the troops, we moved on to the place appointed on the Cahwia river; on my arrival there, I found delegations had already arrived on the ground from some five or six tribes, and others were expected.... I found them willing to treat... and on the 13th of May the treaty was formally signed, &c.

The country given up by these tribes, or some of them, embraces some of the best lands in California, being a portion of what is known in this part of the State as the "Four creek country." The country given to them is generally inferior, but has a sufficiency of good soil, water, &c., to answer all their purposes for all time to come. After agreeing upon the terms of the treaty, but before it had been drawn up and signed, I despatched runners to the other tribes north of Kearn river, and desired them to meet me on Paint creek, at a point designated, about forty miles south from our camp, on the Cahwia. By forced marches, we reached the place designated on the evening of the 1st of June....Those tribes number about two thousand.... I found them more intelligent, more athletic, and better qualified for either peace or war, than any Indians I have seen in California. They were a terror to the Spaniards, being greatly their superiors in war; they have great influence over the neighboring tribes, and until very recently have been at war with the Cahwia and other tribes inhabiting the "Four creek" country. On the 3d of June I concluded a treaty with them....

Having treated with all the tribes between the Sierra Nevada and the "coast range" north of Kearn river, and learning that there were several tribes near the terminus of the Tulare valley, and south of Kearn river, I immediately despatched runners to them, requesting them to meet me at the Texan (Tahone) Pass, about seventy-five miles distant from Paint creek. I reached the Pass, at the southern extremity of the Tulare valley, on the night of the 6th; on the 7th the chiefs and captains of eleven tribes or bands, with the most of their people, came in; and on the 10th, I concluded a treaty with them, which was formally signed, &c.; a copy of which I also enclose herewith to you. This treaty embraced the last of the tribes in the San Joaquin and Tulare valleys, from the Stanislaus river north to the Los Angelos south, including the whole country from the top of the Sierra Nevada to the coast, embracing a district of country from four to five hundred miles in length, and from one hundred and fifty to two hundred in width.

The tribes included in the last treaty were mostly small bands, mere remnants of tribes once large and powerful; but, what with the drafts made upon them by the Spanish missions, (several of which are located just across the mountains, within the immediate vicinity,) for laborers, and the almost exterminating wars that, from time to time, have been carried on among themselves, together with the ravages of disease *intentionally* [53] spread among them by the Spaniards who feared them, they have, in some instances, been almost annihiliated. The Uvas, once among the most powerful tribes in the valley, have been, by such means, reduced to a mere handful, and do not now number more than twenty persons; and among the Texans [Tejons], I met with an *old man*, the last of his tribe, at one time a large and powerful tribe, but war and

[53] An unwarranted accusation.

pestilence had done their work, and *he alone* was left to prove that such a tribe had once existed....

[*Report of the Commissioner of Indian Affairs*, 1851, pp. 493-98.]

*

INDIANS AND AGUA[R]DIENTE

An examination took place on Tuesday last, before Justice Burrill, of four Indians, charged with stealing a barrel of aguadiente and a cloak, the property of Mr. Keller. The Indians confessed the theft and were sentenced to be whipped, twenty-five lashes each, and to pay the expenses of the prosecution.

[Los Angeles *Star*, July 17, 1852.]

*

FROM THE TULARE VALLEY

A party of men who have been prospecting through the Tulare Valley, arrived in town yesterday. They report that at the Four Creeks they found the Indians very insolent, but had no serious trouble with them. There were some eight white men living about the Four Creeks, and forming a settlement for farming purposes. Several days after our informants left the Four Creeks, some Indians came into their camp and reported that the eight white men above alluded to had been all killed by the Tulare Indians. An attempt was made to return and ascertain the truth of the report, but the guides (friendly Indians) who evidently placed confidence in the statement, declined conducting them back, and the party came on to this city. We give the story as we heard it, but if there is truth in it, we shall learn more in the course of a few days.

[Los Angles *Star*, July 17, 1852.]

*

Recent information from the Tulare Valley leads us to believe that the whites at the Four Creeks have destroyed several rancherias in that vicinity, and that the rumor of the Indians having murdered eight white men there, as published last week, was premature.

[Los Angeles *Star*, July 24, 1852.]

*

CALIFORNIA INDIANS

The light that has been thrown upon the history of the Indians of Los Angeles county, in the interesting letters [by Hugo Reid] published in a series in the *Star*, must have a practical tendency to ameliorate their condition. No doubt every philanthropist, upon the perusal of those letters has asked, if nothing can be done for the prospective and permanent welfare of this unfortunate race. In taking up this subject, I hope to suggest such measures as will secure the prospective good of the Indians of this Southern part of California.

I regard the policy pursued by Agents of the General Government towards our Indians as being at war with the interests of the people and of the Indians themselves. That policy has crazed the heads of the leaders of the different tribes, induced pride, self-importance and clan-ships, which had almost ceased to exist; and had broken in upon the former order of things. It has led to the abandonment of the ranchos and pueblos by the Indians almost entirely, each petty chief calling in the straggling members of his tribe from fields of labor, to swell his own importance by a show of numbers. Such is the case with the Cahuillas and their chief, Juan Antonio, and other tribes. The policy referred to, by affording sufficient provisions to the Indians to live upon without work, has created a grand "fiesta"; and the Indian servants have generally left their employers to gather to the festival; and idleness and consequent crime and outrage will be the result. Indian leaders are rising in their own importance and that of their people; tribes which had almost ceased to exist are being collected together from all the neighboring ranchos and pueblos, and by concentration becoming more formidable. The very feeding of them by the government, without the necessity of work, has become the most potent cause of their being daily rendered more formidable.

The lands which have been set apart to them favor the return of the Indian servants scattered over the country, to nationality separate, independent and superior to our State laws. Already have complaints arisen as to these lands, which are every day increasing, and will ultimately lead to collision and bloodshed. Before the arrival of the government agents, such a thing as property in lands had not entered the minds of our California Indians. To be sure, some few instances existed of Indians quite civilized, whose claims to, and cultivation of lands, were respected; but these were rare. Now, the idea having been implanted in the minds of the Indians, they will pertenaciously cling to the grants which have been laid out and given to their tribes.

Such have been a few of the mistakes and injuries inflicted upon us. If Government was aware of the true state of things, the policy already begun would undoubtedly be changed.

The State of California has, from the first, treated the Indians as citizens, not sufficiently enlightened to have all the privileges of the citizens, to wit: in regard to the elective franchise, and giving evidence against their white neighbors; but in all other respects, and to all intents and purposes, citizens. The idea of them as distinct tribes or petty nationalities, within the territory of the State, did not occur to the framers of our Constitution and Legislature, for the facts were all contrary to such hypothesis. All Indians within our territory were required to render implicit obedience to our laws and respect to our officers, and were guaranteed the protection of the same.

Nor had the Indians any idea of a government among themselves that was not in direct subjection to our government
and laws. These facts are fully sustained by the Constitution,
the Statute concerning the government and protection of Indians, passed April 22d, 1850, and by the uniform obedience
of the Indians, in all judicial proceedings under said laws up
to the present time. To show the policy of our State towards
the Indians, we quote from the statute:

"1. Justices of the Peace shall have jursidiction *in all cases*
of complaints by, for, or against Indians in their respective
townships in this State.

"2. Persons and proprietors of lands on which Indians are
residing, shall permit such Indians peaceably to reside on
such lands, unmolested in the pursuit of their usual avocations for the maintenance of themselves and families, &c.

"3. Any person having, or hereafter obtaining a minor Indian, male or female, from the parent or relation of such Indian
minor, and wishing to keep it, such person shall go before a
Justice of the Peace, in his township, [who] shall give such
person a certificate, authorizing him or her to have the care,
custody, control and earnings of such a minor, until he or she
obtain the age of majority."

In the next section the guardian is bound to clothe, feed,
and properly treat such minor.   PHILO.

(To be continued.)⁵⁴

[Los Angeles *Star*, August 14, 1852.]

*

E. F. BEALE TO B. D. WILSON

San Francisco, October 8, 1852

Enclosed I send you a commission as one of the Indian Agents
for the State of California.

⁵⁴ The August 21 issue, which presumably had the second installment
of this paper, has not been preserved.

You will see by the enclosed extracts from the letters of the Comr. of Indn. Affs. that your Salary will commence from the execution of your Bond & oath of office.

Immediately on the fulfilment of these obligations you will transmit the bond to this office for approval and transmission to Washington.

It is impossible at this distance to direct your movements, and I therefore defer giving you instructions, until a personal interview and a visit to the Southern tribes puts me in possession [of] a full knowledge of our affairs in that part of the State.

(P. S.) You will execute the enclosed bond in the Penal sum of $5000. with two or more securities whose sufficiency must be attested by a United States Judge or District Attorney.

[Wilson Papers, Huntington Library.]

*

A. C. RUSSELL TO B. D. WILSON

San Francisco, October 15 [1852]

... It gives me pleasure to congratulate you on your appointment to the Indian Agency. I bespeak a place on your "staff" the first trip you make to the mountains....

[Wilson Papers, Huntington Library.]

*

THE NEW INDIAN COMMISSIONER

The universal expression of satisfaction at the appointment of Mr. Benj. D. Wilson to the office of Indian Commissioner is the surest evidence that the appointment is a good and proper one. Mr. Wilson is thoroughly acquainted with the Indian character, and has visited most, if not all, the tribes within one hundred miles of this point. In occasions of difficulty between themselves he is always looked to as a mediator, and scarcely a week passes that does not bring some of the chiefs to his residence, invoking his aid and protection. Mr. Wilson accepts the office as much from a desire to secure peace and justice to the Indians, as from a disposition to render to the government of the United States whatsoever service may be in his power. We regard the appointment as securing permanent peace with all those tribes which have, in times past, been so troublesome to this country.

[Los Angeles *Star*, October 16, 1852.]

*

THE TULARES

Two of the chiefs of the Tulare Indians have been in town during the past week, endeavoring to seek redress for some alleged aggressions committed by their white neighbors. They say that some white people have encroached upon their grounds near the Four Creeks and have taken prisoners several of their children. Mr. Wilson, to whom their complaints were made, dismissed them with the promise that he would look into the matter and would use his endeavors to see them righted.

[Los Angeles *Star*, October 16, 1852.]

*

JURUPA

An indian boy named Felipe Valdez, was brought before Luis Robideux, the Justice of the Peace at Jurupa, on the 13th inst. charged with stealing $40, a pistol and a bottle of whiskey. He confessed the charge, and was thereupon sentenced by the Justice to receive thirteen lashes. The sentence was duly carried into effect.

[Los Angeles *Star*, October 30, 1852.]

*

LO, THE POOR INDIAN

When the Indian Appropriation Bill was before Congress last session, the House of Representatives cut down from 120,000 to 20,000 dollars, an appropriation which the Senate had adopted for protecting the Indians in California. A committee of conference was chosen between the Senate and House, of which Mr. Gwin of California, was chairman. Mr. Gwin, in making his report to the Senate, said:

"I must be permitted to express the mortification which I experienced at the ignorance displayed by those who represented the House on this committee, of the subject matter of our discussions—an ignorance that I fear, if permitted to rule the proceedings of that House, will prove disastrous to the best interests of the State I in part represent here." Mr. Gwin said farther, in speaking of the necessity of making provision for the protection of the California Indians:

"*We have taken their acorns, grasshoppers, fisheries, and hunting grounds from them.* The ponds where the wild fowl assembled in the winter, offering them for the time an abundant supply of food, is now the mining and agricultural region of our citizens. The Indian must perish from cold and hunger if this Government does not interpose to save him. From his hunting-ground we export an annual average of $60,000,000 in gold, and the revenue paid to the Treasury, from one port in California, exceeds $3,000,000 annually; and yet the miserable pittance of 120,000 to feed and protect these original inhabitants of the country, is refused and cut down to 20,000 dollars, by the grossly unjust policy adopted by the other House. If this is to be the policy of this Government towards this people, it will form a dark page in our history, if it does not bring the vengeance of heaven upon us as a nation."

[Los Angeles *Star*, October 30, 1852.]

*

B. D. WILSON TO [E. F. BEALE]

San Francisco, November 11, 1852

In reply to your communication bearing the same date of this, upon Examining the Invoice of Indian goods sent to you by the Govt. for presents to the Indians in California, first the Greater part of the goods are intirely useless such as the Indians do not use Consequently not worth moveing from San Francisco the other part say the cloths shawls & calicos though not the articles wanted may answer some purpose & I must say that my conviction is that the purchase was a bad one what our Indians want is something to eat, & ware such as common Blankets brown domestic &c but the principal with the Indians is something to Eat as in our climate clothing is a secondary consideration with the Indians.

[Signed draft, Wilson Papers, Huntington Library.]

*

E. F. BEALE TO B. D. WILSON

San Francisco, November 22, 1852

You will assist this office, by giving me your opinion, as to the Section of Indian country most needing protection, and also as to the best means of shielding the Los Angeles district from Indian depredations.

[Wilson Papers, Huntington Library.]

*

B. D. WILSON TO E. F. BEALE

San Francisco, November 22, 1852

In reply to your request Respecting Indian affairs. In the Southern portion of this State we consider the Indians commonly called the four creek Indians of the first Importance for the reasons as follows these Indian ocupy a central position in the Southern district of this State & consiquently they Exercise a great influence over the other detached tribes living more Immeadeately upon our frontiers those Indians of the four creeks is the strong hold of all the San Joaquin Valey as well as the other mountain tribes living adjacently to them. Though we have a large number of Indians commonly called the Cahuilla Indians & San Luis Indians living upon our South Eastern borders still these Indian are Easily managed as they always have had & necessarily must have a great intercourse with our Inhabitants & are more disposed to be friendly. We have a large number Indians liveing upon the *rio Colorado* these Indians do little or no mischief in our State. they are a great annoyance to the Imigration and the travilling community.

[Wilson Papers, Huntington Library.]

*

BENJAMIN HAYES TO
SENATOR DAVID R. ATCHISON OF MISSOURI

[Los Angeles] January 14, 1853

At this time I wish to say a word or two touching on Indian Affairs. Let me beg you to notice the Report of the Indian agent for this District, Benjamin D. Wilson, Esq. I am acquainted, of my own knowledge, with nearly all the facts stated by him concerning the character of these Indians, the country they live in, their troubles for the last three years and the causes of them. I have travelled over a great part of their country and camped in it. My opportunities have been various and constant for observing them. And I have given no little attention to the subject—more I suspect, than any other resident here, unless I except Mr. Wilson.

A man who has never mixed with these Indians, can have no idea of the utter difference between them and those of the Great Plains—whose character for the chase and war has so long baffled the benevolent designs of the Government. This

Report ought to be printed by Congress and circulated generally in this State and elsewhere. It presents the true plan for managing these Indians. And the boldness with which he asserts the legal right of the Mission Indians to their property, in the face of the *speculators* in Mission titles, some of them otherwise his bosom friends, might immortalize some men, even of greater ability and in a higher station.

I am partly induced to write this letter—without his knowledge (for I shall not show it to him) by having heard this evening, that some half dozen worthy men who suppose the whole weight and responsibility of the different officers here is upon their shoulders, think of getting up a sort of recommendation of Don *Antonio F. Coronel,* for this office. I know him intimately, respect him, and would do any thing reasonable to advance his interests. He has been assessor of this county, is rather popular, clever and sprightly, has been active as a Democrat in the two political elections we have had here as yet—supported *me* warmly. But, I cannot conscientiously favor him for this responsible post. He is a Mexican by birth, but has been in California some years; he is not a "native Californian." So that his appointment would be no extrordinary complement to the "native Californians" (as they are called.) They might be flattered by something of the kind, for the matter of "nine days" or so; if any letters from here assert differently, I assure you, it's mere *stuff.*

I know the "Californians" well. And all of them who would not associate with the idea of an Indian Agent the sole prospect of *dividing out the Indians by force to work on the ranchos,* would infinitely prefer some competent American to one of their own number, under present circumstances.

Candidly, this office ought to be filled by an American, or somebody who can speak English. This seems to be a *sine qua non.* They are to be reared to the uses of American Civilization which cannot be easily separated from the language in which it expresses itself. Mr. Coronel does not write, read, or speak English. It is no desparagement of his other qualities, to say, frankly, that he has not that degree of *moral courage* requisite for an Indian agent in California. There is an absolute necessity of having men here, of iron firmness, to execute the laws, without respect to local caprices, or interests, or prejudices. I do not believe the Indian intercourse laws can be enforced here, by any but an American against Americans (of whom there may be plenty to violate them.) This is a daily experience, in judicial and other proceedings. Generally speaking, a "Californian" will not accept an office to which any similar responsibility is attached. You could not get one, for example, to run for Sheriff or constable—not because he could not be elected; but for the reason, that he naturally shuns civil positions of difficulty or danger.

Besides, if you have such an Agent, all your sub-agents, must be of the same class. Americans will not be under the control of such an Agent. They will either resign, or they will control him; which, I suppose is not the spirit of the law. The last would be the result invariably, and any system whatsoever become full of abuses. I should tremble for the poor Indian subjected to them.

Moreover, grave questions are agitated in relation to the rights of these Indians—and of many white persons—under the old law in force here concerning the Missions, etc. The men who took part in public transactions from 1834 to July, 1846, in California, might be good witnesses, in regard to them, but I will ask in sober earnest, would they be the best judges, or would they make the proper representatives of the rights and interests of others, which their own acts as legis-

lators or otherwise, whether of omission or commission, may
have directly affected?

The condition of the Indians during the period referred to,
is a black page of history. I believe, Mr. Coronel then was
never more than *Alcalde*. But it is readily seen, the Government needs men without even that connection with so unfortunate an epoch of Indian misrule, oppression, and injustice.
There is more in this objection than I can conveniently put
to paper.

Mr. Wilson is an old mountaineer, and a gentleman in every sense of the word. He is wealthy and independent—and
so does not need this office. His wealth has come to him in a
measure suddenly, by the rise of property; after many "hard
knocks" in the Rocky Mountains and here, before, during and
since the war. He has been in some little campaigns formerly
against portions of these Indians, and knows them, and they
know him well. Before his appointment, their Chiefs visiting
the City, habitually came to see and talk with him about their
business, as much as if he were their Agent. Notoriously he
is a favorite with them—no stranger. His good sense, kindness of heart, knowledge of mountain life, familiarity with all
the tribes, and reputation for integrity of purpose, are difficult to combine in any one else that may be recommended
from this quarter. He reminds me a good deal of old Maj.
Cummings, of Westport, Mo.

It would be good policy to keep him in this office, at any
rate until some efficient plan is put in operation for the benefit of these Indians: the difficulty of making any plan work
well is at the beginning. A removal ought not to be made pre-
maturely, or hastily.

There are many men watching these Indians—some Democrats (so-called) among them—but to make them the prey

of a grand *speculation*. Think, for instance, of "beef cattle" at $75 per head—when they can be furnished slaughtered at any point you want them, where the Indians live, at $30 per head—and this, with a princely profit. Let care be taken, by inquiry into the position of men, lest such may not be one of the principal objects of some recommendations from here for the appointment of Agent.

A receiving agent lately gave a receipt for 1000 head of cattle. I am credebly informed, the Indians deny the receipt of more than 300 head. This was under one of the rejected treaties.

In one of his speeches Mr. Gwin has shown admirably how much California has been injured at Washington, by this extravagance and by unnecessary expenditures.[55]

[Draft, Hayes Scrapbooks, Bancroft Library, XXXIX, 121.]

*

INDIAN MATTERS

We have been permitted to examine the report of B. D. Wilson, Esq., Indian Commissioner for the Southern District of California, upon the condition of the Indians coming particularly under his supervision. Besides the statistical and other valuable information contained in the report, it suggests a plan for the future government of the Indians, strictly philanthropic, and which, if carried out, cannot fail to benefit a people once more than half civilized, but now exhibiting such signs of retrogression and decay as must be deplored by every humane heart.

[55] A further extract from Hayes' letter to Atchison, January 14, 1853, is preserved in his diary:

"After considering the report of Mr. Wilson, if the President thinks a man of such sentiments ought to be removed, let it be done. But I do trust the utmost caution will be observed in choosing his successor. He claims to be a Whig. One of a rather mild stamp, as he strikes my eye, and not very dangerous to Democracy. A man is not apt to be much of

After giving a sketch of each tribe, their habits, customs, etc., at present and also under the Mission system, Mr. Wilson recommends the following plan for their management:

It is proposed that the lands within the following boundaries be reserved for the use of the different Indian tribes now inhabiting those regions: A line drawn from the eastern boundary of Santa Isabel direct to the N. E. corner of the Laguna rancho, (thereby including Temecula and Agua Caliente,) thence along the northern boundary of Laguna, so as to include the San Jacinto rancho and the tract commonly known as San Gorgonio—the whole distance, say 100 miles; thence in a direct course 80 miles to the Tejon, (including the rancho of that name;) thence 100 miles to the Four Creeks; the remainder of the boundary to be completed by running a line due south, say 40 miles, from Santa Isabel to the boundary between Mexico and the United States. The respective limits of this boundary could be defined as conveniently as counties are elsewhere. Not one thousand acres of this territory are now occupied by the cattle or crops of white men, and only two white men now reside upon any part of it. The Mexican claims can be quieted for a reasonable sum, and more easily than the Indian title can be extinguished. At the present time these lands are mere wastes, as far as the hand of man has anything to do with them.

Mr. Wilson recommends one principal town or pueblo at

a politician who has not been in 'the States' for nineteen years, and has been roughing it all that time in mountains and deserts. I assure you that there are not a dozen of the six hundred Democrats in this county who really desire any change in this office, believing that it is now in experienced and faithful hands. If I had time, I might back these suggestions with the concurrent signatures of nearly all the people of Southern California."

[*Pioneer Notes* (Los Angeles, 1929), 97.]

each reserve. There would be eight towns, one at each of the following places: At the Four Creeks, the Tulareños, about 1000 Indians; at the Tejon, Tulareños, 1000; San Gorgonio, Cahuillas, 1500; San Jacinto, Cahuillas, 1500; Temecula, San Luiseños, 1000; Agua Calientes, Diegueños, 1000; Mouth of Gila, Yumas, 1000; and on the Upper Colorado, Mohaves, 1000. The establishment of towns at the Gila and Colorado might be delayed for some time and until the working of the system should prove to be advantageous.

It is estimated that 1000 head of cattle, with their own natural resources, would be sufficient to support them six months; the cattle could be delivered slaughtered, at the villages, for $30,000. Then too, they would require a small supply of clothing, blankets, &c. After the first six months, they would not only support themselves, but have a surplus. They have done this before, and would do it again. The productions should be kept common stock, and dealt to them in daily or tri-weekly rations—The lands of each town should also be held as common lands, until it became expedient to dispose otherwise; individual concessions might be made to the more industrious.

The immediate control of the affairs of each village would be entrusted to an agent appointed specially for the purpose. The agent could give permission to some of the Indians to bind themselves out to the rancheros for a term not to exceed one year, but as a general thing the Indians would be required to reside in their respective territories. A blacksmith, carpenter, and farmer should be employed for each village, to teach the Indians agriculture and the mechanic arts; and schools for the instruction of the young should be established upon some uniform system. It is thought the expense of carrying into successful operation the mode of government suggested by

Mr. Wilson, will not exceed the cost of one of the numerous expeditions which have been undertaken against the Indians since the organization of our state government.

The report contains a vast fund of information, and the publication of it will be an important addition to the cause of science. The views of Mr. Wilson touching the management of the Indians become important at this time, when the whole course of Legislation seems tending towards the extermination of the Indian race. If the government of the U. States desires the preservation of the Indians, some system must be adopted similar to that proposed by Mr. Wilson. It could be put in operation here most effectually, for the various tribes hereabout have a vivid recollection of the "good old days" of the Missions, and they desire now, more than ever before, the protection and care of their white neighbors.

[Los Angeles *Star*, January 15, 1853 (clipping in Hayes Scrapbooks, XXXVIII: 121).]

*

PRAISEWORTHY

The wretched, worthless wo-begone Indians who, as regularly as Sunday comes around, occupy our city prison on charges varying from drunkenness to stealing, making disturbances in the streets, stabbing, &c., were last Monday employed by the city authorities in the healthful and benevolent occupation of clearing away the rubbish which has been accumulating for a long time in the streets, and the result of their labors is certainly an improvement in the general aspect of affairs. The plan adopted seems to be [an] admirable one, and it is to be hoped it will be continued. If Indians *will* get drunk and kick up a row, why let them work it out. If white men do the same, why—"let 'em rip."

[Editorial, Los Angeles *Star*, February 12, 1853.]

*

JUSTIN McKINSTRY TO BENJAMIN HAYES

San Diego, February 25, 1853

I have not the pleasure of a personal acquaintance with B. D. Wilson Esq, Indian Agent resident in your city, but have written to him Soliciting his Kind assistance and co-operation in my endeavors to prepare for publication a Memoir of the Missions & Indians of this State. Will you do me the favor to call upon him and endeavor to induce his assistance. If so I will take it as a very great personal favor. We have nothing new. Old town is dying of ennui.

P. S. During the past year a series of articles on the Indians by Hugo Reid, I am told appeared in the Star. Will you be kind enough to procure & send copies to me?

[Wilson Papers, Huntington Library.]

*

RUMORS FROM SAN GORGONIO

Frequent rumors reach our city from San Gorgonio, that the Indians are deprived of the use of the water, by Mr. Weaver, and that in consequence they are unable to sow their grain. We hope the rumors may not prove true; for the acts complained of are outrages which may provoke retaliation. The law expressly provides that the Indians shall retain uninterrupted possession of lands they may have occupied for a series of years. Moreover, these Indians are Juan Antonio's Cahuillas, with whom Gen. Bean formed a treaty, pledging the faith of the State that they should not be molested so long as they observed its terms. Thus, to deprive them of any of their former privileges would be a violation of both the law and the treaty, and may lead to serious difficulties. We hope Mr. Weaver appreciates the importance of maintaining inviolate the pledged faith of the State with these Indians, and the dangers he may incur by provoking them to hostilities.

[Los Angeles *Star*, February 26, 1853.]

*

HORSES STOLEN AND RECOVERED

We have a rumor, the truth of which is well attested, that a few days since, a band of Pah-Utahs stole two bands of horses, from the rancho of Ignacio Palomares. They were pursued and the horses retaken except five, which the Indians had killed for food. The Pah-Utahs are wild Indians of the Desert. They are expert thieves, and are under no control of our government. This band of Indians are said to be, at present, in the San Fernando Valley.

[Los Angeles *Star*, February 26, 1853.]

*

B. D. WILSON TO BENJAMIN HAYES

Los Angeles, February 27, 1853

My official Duties at present require my presents in los Angeles County as I have Several appointments made to see the different Captains of the different tribes north & south of this City. I am also apprised of the necessity of the presence of some authorized person among Indian Villages of San Diego County who might be of Great Service at this time Especially giving them some tools & other little presents to facilitate there planting &c. They being no sub-agents appointed as yet for these two counties and it not being in my power for the reasons given above to visit San Diego for some time to come am feeling anxious that nothing Shall remain undone that comes under my Jurisdiction and being informed that you on your official Duty leave in a few days for that place and as I Know of no person in whom I have more implicit confidence than yourself and that you have as much or more acquaintance than almost any other person with these Indians —I hereby appoint you to act as Sub-Agent during your stay in San Diego County and request & hope you will visit all the villiges in your power & make such distributions among the

Indian as in your judgment may be done with limited me[ans]
that I am prepared to give to you for that purpose (Three hundred dollars) Hoping you will be so kind as to report on your
return all the information relative to the Indians that comes
under your observation during your absence

[Draft, Wilson Papers, Huntington Library.]

✳

In our last number we reported certain thefts of horses made
by the wild Indians, but we did not mention a large number
of horses and broken mules stolen at the same time from Don
Julian [Isaac] Williams without a one being recovered, and a
considerable number from Don Ignacio Palomares, of which,
although most were retaken, the rest were lost by the arrows
of the Indians.

A few days later, they stole from Don Juan Ávila eight
horses that were tied near [Williams'] house on the ranch,
and with these they ran off one hundred and fifty animals, and,
although these were recovered, many were lost in the same
manner as with Palomares' horses. On Friday of last week
they stole a herd of more than a hundred horses from Don J.
Serrano and the next day about fifty saddle horses from Don
Juan Ávila.

As soon as he had the news, Don Juan Fo[r]ster gathered
a force of thirty men from among the neighboring rancheros
and set off in pursuit of the Indian raiders. Following their
trail by the horses which the Indians left killed by their arrows, they entered the range of Santiago, [but] because of
nightfall lost the trail. On this account they decided to go to
the northern side of the range and wait for the Indians to come
out. At dawn Fo[r]ster's party joined that of Don Juan Ávila
and José Sepulveda, which had been pursuing the earlier raid-

ers for a week. Together the parties formed a force of about fifty men. They proceeded to take the most active measures for another six days. But notwithstanding these efforts, they could not find a sign of the last band of robbers, due to the fact that the Indians had discovered a new route different from the usual ones.

After this time lost, the neglect of their affairs, the leaving of their families exposed to the risk of another attack by the savages, and having lost hope of getting revenge, they returned home to wait until the Indians should come back for the few horses they had left and perhaps to kill them and their families.

We call this to the attention of our representatives in order that in the ways and means which they consider convenient it may be made clear that the Indians who despoil this county are distant tribes, not the peaceful Indians who are in our vicinity. It is very sad that after the payment of enormous taxes our lives and properties are not secure.

[*La Estrella*, April 2, 1853.[56]]

*

THE INDIANS AGAIN

We last week published two communications on the subject of the recent thieving incursions of the Pah Utahs in this county; one from Mr. Wilson, the Government agent, the other from a gentleman who has suffered by the loss of stock, giving an account of the stealing of a cavallada of horses from Col. Williams.[57] This week, also, reports have been every day brought into town of continued robberies, but so vague and indefinite are most of them, that we do not care to publish all

[56] Translated from the Spanish section of the Los Angeles *Star*. The story is based on information from Isaac Williams.

[57] The preceding number for March 26 has not been preserved, but see the preceding item.

the details. We all know this, however, that the depredations of the Indians are a great annoyance to our farmers; that they are fast draining the wealth of the county in more respects than one, not only in the amount of stock stolen, but the insecurity which is felt by all is a great hindrance to successful farming and grazing operations, and occasions an additional expense in the care of the animals. We have suffered a long time from this source, during which we have had several "Indian Wars," the result of each of which has been a vast addition to the debt of our already deeply involved States; several "straw" treaties, which amount to nothing at all, unless, indeed, they serve to keep the fires of discord continually kindled by the examples which they furnish each party of the treachery and unfaithfulness of the other, and a feeling of insecurity and want of confidence in any Government or State force, to afford protection or redress. Military stations we have, to be sure, but the troops are all infantry, and of course of about as much use as a padlock without a key. Of the amount of *negative* good they accomplish we cannot judge, but we know the positive benefit which they afford is just none at all.

In view of these facts, and our present situation, we confess that, however unprecedented or bold it may appear to some, the plan proposed by Mr. Wilson, seems to us to be the only one by which we can better our condition; and it is so feasible, and can be accomplished with so little expense, that we should like to see it carried into effect at once. We are informed that the Indians who make these forays are but about one hundred in number, and that a detachment of from ten to fifteen only, come in at a time. They inhabit a place to the north of the Tejon Pass, about six days journey from this city. A party of fifty to seventy five men could easily proceed to their camp, give them a whipping—one too, that they would remember —and get back again in two or three weeks.

Now that the proposition has been broached, it remains for those interested to carry it into effect. The rancheros and farmers are the ones who suffer. Let them turn out as strong as possible, and should they lack in numbers, we doubt not plenty of men could be found to assist them, were they furnished with animals; and a blow can be struck, the effects of which will be salutary and lasting.

[Los Angeles *Star*, April 2, 1853.]

*

RAPE

Juan, an Indian, was cited before Justice Dryden on Thursday, on a charge of rape committed on the person of a California woman, named Juana Ivarra. The woman testified that she was returning to the rancho de Arollo Seco, her home, on the 18th ult., and that when a short distance from town, the Indian came up with her, and after almost completely divesting her of her clothing, rudely assaulted and finally violated her person. The accused was committed to jail, there to await the action of the Grand Jury upon the same. The Grand Jury meets on the 4th inst.

[Los Angeles *Star*, April 2, 1853.]

*

INDIAN VISIT

About 100 Indians from San Luis Rey honored our city with a visit yesterday. They came for the purpose of paying their respects to the Indian Agent, (Indians always have an eye to business) and to collect some presents. In accordance with the authority vested in him, Mr. Wilson distributed some agricultural implements among them, the receipt of which seemed to give them infinite satisfaction.

[Los Angeles *Star*, April 2, 1853.]

*

FRED BUEL TO B. D. WILSON

San Francisco, April 23, 1853

...I see that Wozencraft and McKee are being hauled over the coals by Lt. Beale. I hope the agent at the South will be continued in office and save the country from being cheated and the indians from abuse....

[Wilson Papers, Huntington Library.]

*

INDIAN DEPREDATIONS

Editors of the Star:—Indian depredation, so common in this Southern portion of our State, is a matter of such frequency and importance, that any light upon the subject to the community would no doubt be of interest. About a month ago, when the Indians from the Tejon were here on a visit, I made all the inquiry possible to get information relative to the supposed horse thiefs. They then told me that they knew the Indians that annoyed us so much. I asked them to make a visit to those Indians, as they said they were friendly with each other, which they promised to do. On the second of this month, one of those captains came in to advise me of the result of these visits, which was as follows:

These horse thieves inhabit the region of country bounded on the north by Owen's Lake, and on the head branches of Kerne river, about three days' travel from the Tejon, in a northeasterly direction. They are a small tribe, not supposed to number over fifty warriors. The captains of these thiefes told the Tejon Indians that the parties which steal horses, are headed by two renegade Indians, who have each about seven or eight young men that follow them, and that these two divide their time so as one can come every new moon; and that they always take animals. They kill a large portion of them, and sell the balance to Indians living north [of] Owen's lake. They also sell to the American emigrants, for blankets, &c.

The Tejon Indians assure me that the captains of these thieves, are opposed to these indians' stealing; and are, as they believe, disposed to give up the principal thieves for punishment. And the Tejon Indians have now promised to go, in a large body, on another visit, and try to capture the thieves. They say if they fail that they would like to join a party of Americans and go and take them. They say by going by the Tejon that they will go as guides, and that there is good grass and water every night. That these Indians are easy of access, and can be easily captured by a small party. That the way they have usually been pursued, down the Mojave river, is much farther and a bad country, neither water nor grass, and on that route, they always manage to elude their pursuers.

I am satisfied that the above statement is about correct; and I am also satisfied that any treaty made with these Indians, without their first feeling our power, would be of no avail.— How easy for those interested to make up a party and pay them a visit, and convince them that they can no longer steal with impunity.   B.D.W.

[Los Angeles *Star*, May 7, 1853.]

*

BETTER TIMES

There were fewer drunken Indians seen about the streets last Saturday than is usual on that day, and in consequence it passed off without the noise and brawling which are apt to characterize our Sabbaths. The credit of this change for the better is due to our new City Marshal, Mr. Beard,who, since his election has been untiring in his efforts to preserve order and discharge all the duties which his office imposes upon him. He has been particularly "down" upon that portion of our community who make their living by selling liquor to the Indians, and we hope he will continue in his exertions to bring all such to an account. If he can succeed in removing this

fruitful source of trouble and disgrace, he will richly deserve
the thanks of the community.

[Editorial, Los Angeles *Star*, May 14, 1853.]

*

BY FORCE OF HABIT

Juan Gonzalis was brought before Justice Dryden last Tuesday, on a charge of selling intoxicating liquor to Indians, and
was allowed to depart after a short conference with his honor,
by a fine of twenty dollars and costs—in all $41. His excuse
was that he had "got into the habit of doing it." Our new City
Marshal has kindly volunteered to assist in breaking him of
the "habit," for which Mr. Gonzalis should be, and doubtless is, duly grateful.

During the whole week our vigilant District Attorney has
been very active in prosecuting cases of the above class. A.W.
Timms was fined $20 and costs for selling liquor to Indians,
and Peter Collins for a like offence was mulched in the same
amount:—all, before Judge Burrell. Alexander Ramon was
complained of on two separate charges of same nature, on
each of which he was convicted and fined $20 and costs.
Eugene Agaia was also called upon to fork over $20 and costs
for furnishing Indians the wherewith to get drunk, which
amount Judge Dryden received from him on behalf of the
county. To Mr. Beard belongs the credit of bringing these
offenders to an account, and to Attorney Dimmick that of
their earnest and successful prosecution.

Now if Mr. Beard will only overhaul some of the larger establishments, a great deal of whose support is derived from
the same business, and break them up, every good citizen will
be loud in his praise.

[Editorial, Los Angeles *Star*, May 14, 1853.]

*

INDIAN AFFAIRS

Lt. Beale, the Superintendent of Indian affairs in this State, is on his way hither, and may be expected to arrive sometime during the present month, via Walker's Pass. From the law concerning Indian reservations we make the following extract:

"That the President of the United States is authorized to make five military reservations from the public domain in the State of California, or the territories of Utah and N. Mexico bounding on said State, for Indian purposes. Provided that such reservations shall not contain more than 25,000 acres. That such reservations shall not be made upon any lands inhabited by citizens of California, and the sum of $250,000 is hereby appropriated to defray the expense of subsisting the Indians in California, and removing them to said reservations for protection."

The reservations in the Southern part of the State will be selected upon the arrival of Mr. Beale—the immediate agency in connection with the details of the management being entrusted to B. D. Wilson, Esq., of this city. A synopsis of Mr. Wilson's plan for the government of the Indians was published in this paper last winter, and if it is carried out will ensure the welfare of the Indians and the security of the whites living upon our frontiers.

[Los Angeles *Star*, June 4, 1853.]

*

F. E. KERLIN TO B. D. WILSON

San Francisco, June 11, 1853

I wrote you a letter a few days since telling you I would send you some blanks.

With regard to your accounts, it will be necessary for you to be very particular about your vouchers, stating in them the reasons for purchaseing everything, or the reasons for travelling &c. and take vouchers for all moneys you have spent. I enclose to you a blank, for Property Return, should you have any property belonging to the Government. Every article however trifling that is in the vouchers must be accounted for, on this blank. Where any is lost, or broken account for it as so, giving (if possible) a certificate from some disinterested person to that effect. For anything given to the Indians, also send a certificate if possible, and return it as issued to such & such Indians. It is necessary to be very careful of this Return. The next is the Account Current, which you know how to fix. The next, and last is the Abstract of disbursements which is merely an enumeration of the Vouchers. I believe this is all I have to tell you excepting that you are only accountable for $2500. the rest paid you was for Salary & we have your voucher's. If you come up yourself when you send your accounts, and wish any assistance I will give you any in my power with much pleasure.

This is a *Private* letter *not official*.

[Wilson Papers, Huntington Library.]

*

SHOOTING

An Indian suspected of having furnished tools to a prisoner in order to aid his escape, was shot by the jailor Mr. Whitehorne, through the head and leg, yesterday afternoon. The Indian lives, and may recover, the ball having glanced round the skull. We presume there will be a legal investigation of the transaction.

[Los Angeles *Star*, June 18, 1853.]

*

FOUND DEAD

An Indian, named Bacilio, was found dead near the zanja at the upper end of town, this morning. Justice Dryden and a jury sat on the body: verdict, "death from intoxication, or the visitation of God." Bacilio was a Christian Indian and was confessed by the reverend padre, yesterday afternoon.

[Los Angeles *Star*, June 18, 1853.]

*

Hon. J. J. Warner, of San Diego, sends us the following:

On Thursday evening, June 9, about seven o'clock, four men, supposed to be Sonoreños, having with them about forty head of horses, arrived at the rancho of Andres Ibarra, about twenty miles from San Luis Rey, and without provocation fired upon the family, wounding one person in the leg. They then tied three men who were living at the rancho, and after plundering the house of wearing apparel and some money, started off for San Marco, where they killed two bullocks. The following day they were pursued by a party from San Diego until dark, when, being unable to follow the trail, the pursuit was abandoned. Messages were sent to several Indian tribes directing them to capture the marauders. It is supposed that the robbers have gone to the mountains about San Marco to dry their beef. Eight horses were stolen from Santa Margarita on Wednesday one of which was found tied out between Ibarra's and San Marco.

[Los Angeles *Star*, June 18, 1853.]

*

FEROCIOUS

On Thursday last, an Indian attacked an old gentleman named Valdez, inflicting a severe wound with a knife upon the head. Valdez retreated toward the house of Hon. Stephen C. Foster, warding off with his blanket many blows which the Indian struck at him. Mr. Foster and his servant seized and disarmed the Indian, and handed him over to the authorities. He made desperate resistance, striking with his knife at Mr.

Foster, who would without doubt have been wounded had it not been for the timely interference of his servant.

[Los Angeles *Star*, June 18, 1853.]

*

Lieut. Beale, Indian Superintendent in California, has started for the Pacific from St. Louis.[58] The St. Louis *Democrat* says:

He will travel the route indicated by Fremont and Leroux—the Cansar route to the Huerrino, through the Pass El Sangre de Christo, into the head valley of the del Norte, and the Puerto Pass from the valley of San Luis to the waters of the great Colorado of the West, and thence to California by Las Vegas de Santa Clara and Walker's Pass. Superintendent Beale is not employed upon any survey for a road, but merely takes this route as his line of travel in returning to his Superintendency, and finds the greater charm in it because some part of the route is new and its practicability disputed. Col. Benton goes with him to the frontier of Kansas to speak to the people of the Western counties at that place, on the Great Railway project.

[Los Angeles *Star*, June 18, 1853.]

*

LEWIS A. FRANKLIN, *Justice of the Peace*, TO B. D. WILSON

San Diego, August 5, 1853

I send you the accompanying document, as from your position officially, and publicly (as Captn of Rangers) I am led to believe you are in position to see justice done to the Injured Indian, and may prevent not alone, any personal resentment

---

[58] On Beale's journey the principal source is Gwinn Harris Heap, *Central Route to the Pacific...in* 1853 (Philadelphia, 1854). "We obtained fresh horses," runs the description of the last stretch of the trip, "and a gallop of thirty-five miles through a rich and settled country brought us to the city of Los Angeles, where every kindness and attention was shown to us by Mr. Wilson, Indian Agent, and his accomplished lady" (p. 111).

but that engendered hatred between the race of Indians and de razon, which has too frequently been the cause of bloodshed. The men reputed to have committed this gross outrage live in your county, and the only reason that I have not issued a writ of arrest is that I have not had time to have the girl and boy before me under examination so as to constitute a legal charge. So soon however as this can be done all that the Law permits of my doing shall be promptly complied with, ad interim I solicit your investigation into the affair and the same will always be gratefully reciprocated by

[Wilson Papers, Huntington Library.]

*

CAVE J. COUTS, *Subagent, San Diego County,* TO B. D. WILSON
Guajomito Rancho, August 15, 1853

In compliance with your verbal instructions, I have the honor to inform you that, according to the best information I can get, after diligent inquiries, the number of Indians in the County, exclusive of those beyond the Rancho San Jacinto & on the Colorado, cannot be far from *Three Thousand-five hundred.*

Those between San Jacinto, or that region of the County, and the Colorado, you have the better means of judging. But I might safely put the whole number in the County at 5,000 *Souls.*

[Wilson Papers, Huntington Library.]

*

CAVE J. COUTS TO B. D. WILSON
Guajomito Rancho, August 15, 1853

Several of the old Indians here, those who were principals among the Indians in the construction of the magnificent old mission, have asked me "if they could not live in the building until such time as the Govt. may want to use it," or "during the rainy season."

There are a number of these old Indians, with families, who have been sufficiently civilized at the Misn., to command considerable respect with the whites who know them well.

Andres, Pedro, Antonio, Samuel, and others in the immediate vicinity of the building, probably all of whom you know, and treated with great consideration by that portion of our citizens who know them well, for their industry and care, in managing their gardens & little stock. They spent their best days laboring in this building, and as it is unoccupied (except by three soldiers detached from a company at S. Diego) I cannot see but that their request is *very reasonable.*

Their only object seems to be, to live there during the "rainy season," and evince every disposition to leave as soon as notified. In the spring they move off to their garden spots, and there remain under their temporary sheds until their crops are gathered.

If this should meet your approbation, I have no doubt but that upon your application at *Washington*, it would be readily granted.

P.S.The Vineyard difficulty at the Portrero, has been settled.
[Wilson Papers, Huntington Library.]

※

JOEL H. BROOKS TO B. D. WILSON

Tejon, August 20, 1853

We have just received a letter from the four creeks written by the county clerk and sent by an indian, informing us that they have taken up Samuel Lago and examined him before a justice's court on a charge of theft with an attempt to Murder. the charges against him were Sustained by testimony Sufficient to induce the Magistrate to commit him for a hearing before the court of Sessions.

Lago was the leader of the party who attempted to commit

a robbery on the Tajone indians a few days ago by stealing their horses, and were deterred by my timely interference.

The indian runer who brought the letter from the four creeks, States that the Same party on their way up killed an indian and woonded an other Somewheres on Tulare River, this newes he learned on his way to this place, and States that the citizens of Woodvill had not heared of this up to the time of his leaving their.

I Shall Start to the county Seat day after tomorow for the purpose of enquiring into the matter and if they have murdered any indians, I Shall take the necessary Stepps to have them arrested, In the mean time I Shall appear on the part of the State, and in behalf of the indians Against Lago.

I Supose that the way Lago came to be taken up was on account of our Sending up a runer to inform them of what had occured here and the result was that he arrived at Woodville before them and they Succeeded in taking up Lago and getting the two Stolen horses, which are now in the hands of the Sheriff, and will be delivered to their proper owners, on application made by us.

P. S. As I Sent down a Sketch of this affair to Mr. Louis [John A. Lewis] Editor of the Star, you will please Show him this.

[Wilson Papers, Huntington Library.]

*

E. F. BEALE TO GEORGE W. MANYPENNY,
Commissioner of Indian Affairs

Los Angeles, August 22, 1853

... My instructions render it imperative that I should abolish the present agencies, and I shall therefore issue the requisite notice to Mr. Wilson at once, though I shall be obliged to employ him in some other capacity, as it is impossible to dis-

pense with his services at present. He is perfectly indifferent
as to holding office—a gentleman of great wealth and high
standing here—and would only consent to serve from a sin-
cere desire to benefit this portion of the country, in which a
long residence has made his influence with the Indians extremely great. I would add also that he never sought the position of agent, but was appointed by the last administration
without ever knowing it until I sent him his commission. I
shall employ him as temporary assistant to superintend the
removal of Indians and to aid in locating reservations, his
knowledge of the country being perfect, and to use his para-
mount influence to induce the Indians to remove in peace.
Mr. Wilson will only consent to give his assistance in any capacity for a short time, not to exceed next spring. . . .

   [*Report of the Commissioner of Indian Affairs*, 1853, p. 468.]

*

B. D. WILSON TO E. F. BEALE

Los Angeles, August 28, 1853

I have in my possession your official communication bearing
date 22nd Inst. in which you inform me that the Indian Agencies are abolished. but that you require my services as an assistant agent to aid you in effecting your arrangements with
the Indians in this portion of the State; which I acept and I
am at your service to perform any duty you command in the
above service.

   I will prepare my accounts immedeatily and forward them
to your office at San Francisco.

   [Wilson Papers, Huntington Library.]

*

ARRIVAL OF LIEUT. BEALE.

Lieut. Beale, Superintendent of Indian Affairs, arrived in
Los Angeles on the 27th ult., himself and company all being
in fine health. They left Westport, Missouri, on 15th June,

but lost 18 days, in consequence of having upset a canoe, with their arms and equipment, in crossing Grand river, a branch of the Colorado. This accident compelled them to delay at that point, until a new supply could be got from Fort Massachusetts, New Mexico,—a distance back of 400 miles, which Mr. Heath accomplished and returned in 18 days. They traveled with pack mules altogether, having no other provisions than pinole and pemican, and wild game with which their hunter supplied them plentifully every day!

From Fort Massachusetts, they took the route described by Leroux in a statement quoted at length by Col. Benton in a recent letter, and which our readers are referred to: the distance from the Fort to Los Angeles being 1077 miles. Lt. Beale describes it as abounding the whole way, to within 150 miles of Los Angeles, with wood, water, and the most luxuriant pasturage—an easy wagon road, and perfectly practicable for the proposed railroad. They had no guide, who might have enabled them to cut off much of the distance. The distance from Fort Massachusetts to Westport, or Independence, is about 750 miles. They had no trouble with Indians.

On Wednesday last, the Lieut.'s company—nine in all—with B. D. Wilson, Esq., Indian agent for southern California, started for San Francisco, by the Tejon, Tulare Valley, etc., intending to visit the Indians on the route; they expect to return in about a month, to complete the necessary arrangements for establishing a Reserve for the Indians of Los Angeles and San Diego counties, either at San Luis Rey Mission, or Temecula. Too much praise cannot be given to Lt. Beale, for the energy and perseverance which he has shown in conducting his little expedition, so successfully, to its destination—occupying in all only fifty travelling days. We trust fervently, that now we are to have a complete change for the better, in the aspect of Indian affairs for California, which must take place if the efforts of the government and its agents meet with a proper sympathy and consideration, from the people of this state.

[Los Angeles *Star*, September 3, 1853.]

*

B. D. WILSON TO MRS. WILSON

Tejon, September 4, 1853

We have been at this place two days & we have all been perfectly well I feel great anxiety about your health and if it was not for so much anxiety about you I should enjoy my trip well as we find the weather Exceedingly pleasant and plenty of game. Indian all very quite. We have about 50 men camped here all of the serveying party looking out a a rail Road route for the Great Pacific R Road among the party of Serveyors I find Lt. Stoneman of the Army who will leave here tomorrow, for Los Angeles I have told him to call & see you. he is an old acquaintance of mine and very much of a Gentleman. I write you these few lines by some Indians who Mr. Beales sends in for his mules & some provisions you will see Mr. Sanford & have Mr. B. letter sent to Andrew Sublettes as it asked Mr. Sublette to deliver to the Indian the mules immediately as we wish their return as soon as posible we will remain here Six days yet to wait the return of the mules from Los Angeles and in the mean time we have sent out to call in all the bordering tribes and to have a *big Indian talk* with them. Mr. Beale will make this place a reserve for the Indians and a beautiful place it is for that perpose when we get through making the necessary arrangements here for the Indians then we shall make a force march for Stockton and San Francisco from which place I will immediately come to Los Angeles. You will send me ½ dozen shirt, three pair drawers I find I will need more clothing than I expected as we find so many people here

we have to dress often it would be best to buy the clothing at
some store. Send me a pair of pants....
  [Wilson Papers, Huntington Library.]

*

B. D. WILSON TO W. B. T. SANFORD

Tejon, September 4, 1853

We have arrived here perfectfuly safe had a fine trip find every thing well Indians quite Mr. Beale will make a reserve
here at this place being the only place suitable in all this part
of the country I suppose we will have a fight with the pre-
tended owners Dn Ygnacio del Valle and old Aguire of San
Diego but it cant be avoided we will remain here about 8 days
to have a big talk here and consiquently have to wait for the
junta of the Indians but when we leave here we will travel
post haste for San Francisco from where I will return home
immediately.

  We found here a party of about 50 men the Serveying party
of which the bearer of this belonged Mr. Beale has Drawn on
you for some suplies please honor Mr. Williamson the sur-
veyor desires to get a 1000$ in cash on his Draft of deposit at
San Francisco I have promised him that you will do it for
him you can use any money of mine you may have on hand
as they need or will probaly need some things before they get
through their work in the lower country I think to accomodate
them with this money will probably help you in commercial
matters so have have said to them that you would do it without charge should you get the Draft and have no use for it
send it up by the next steamer and I will bring the money
down when I come. write me by the Indians who goes for the
mules that Beale left.

  in the night and in haste
  [Wilson Papers, Huntington Library.]

*

STAMPEDE OF INDIANS

Our worthy Marshal and his energetic assistant last Sunday opened the ponderous gates of the prison and locked up twenty five Indians, all supposed to be drunk; but he no sooner had turned his back than, crash! went the door, and the Indians scattered in every direction, up every street in town. Jack swore, and the Marshal, utterly confounded at the impossibility of heading off so many fugitives, stood solemnly silent, and when the last fugitive had disappeared, gave utterance to a sigh and wended his way homeward.

[Los Angeles *Star*, September 17, 1853.]

*

INDIAN AFFAIRS

E. F. Beale, Superintendent of Indian Affairs for the State of California, and Benjamin D. Wilson, Indian Agent for the Southern District, arrived in this city from Stockton yesterday morning. Messrs. Beale and Wilson were in Tejon Valley two weeks, during which time couriers were dispatched to every part of the surrounding country to acquaint the tribes in that region of the fact of Mr. Beale's presence, and calling upon them to assemble, that he might declare to them the intentions of the U. S. government in relation to their affairs. On the 12th of September the chiefs and delegates of tribes had gathered to the number of 1,045, when a Council was held. Mr. Beale addressed the Indians through Mr. Wilson, who translated his remarks into Spanish, which language is understood by many of the chiefs.

Mr. Beale first spoke to the Indians of his arrival amongst them, and informed them of some of the causes of his delay. He told them that he was glad to see that they were so extensively engaged as they were in the cultivation of the land, and spoke of the immense advantage that would accrue to them from a practice of agricultural pursuits. The object of his coming, he said was to do them good, that he was their friend, and desired to see them all happy, and intended to assist them with every means at his command to become so. The principal means proposed to them was the establishment of the reserves, upon which they were to live, and where they would be free from the encroachments of the white man. For this purpose it was necessary to collect them together, and that they should unite cordially in the furtherance of such measures as he should introduce among them for their benefit. He explained to them the difference between the proposed Indian reserve establishments and the Missions of California, with whose former history they were acquainted. In the Missions they had been required to labor for the benefit of the government and the church; on their reserves they would be laboring for themselves. The whites were encroaching upon them from every quarter, and would continue to do so until their establishments were in operation, when all their rights would be respected. The method of labor was not intended to be burdensome, but would be adapted to their physical capacity. A system of rewards and punishments was to be arranged by themselves for their own government and protection. Their captains and head men were to be chosen by themselves.

Mr. Beale spoke to them of the folly of family feuds and jealousies so common among Indian tribes; while mingling with the whites they could never rise to an equal station with them; but among themselves a firm feeling of friendship and equality could exist. He explained to them that, under no circumstances, could he possibly derive any individual benefit from their labor, but that he was the chief among them and should labor to promote their interests. Their organization upon the reserves would be beneficial, not alone to themselves, but they would be building up pleasant homes for their children, where they could live in peace and happiness, reaping the benefits of the labors of the present generation. Here they could build up a city and educate their children for future usefulness.

Mr. Beale informed them that until they should have so far advanced as to be able to support themselves by their labor, assistance would be rendered them by the government, and that they need be under no apprehension of suffering from want. Hunting and fishing were to be allowed them, and although for the present their property and crops were to be as common stock, the ultimate intention was to allow a piece of land to each family.

As there probably were among them many Christian Indians who had been in the missions, provision should be made for their spiritual wants. The padres, he explained to them, however, were not to be allowed any control over temporal affairs.

The alternative was offered them of acquiescence in the will of the Government, or extermination by disease and mixture with the white race. The Council continued two days, at the end of which time the tribes agreed to accept the propositions of the Government made to them by Mr. Beale. Ploughs and other agricultural implements, as well as some stock, are to be furnished them, when they will commence moving on to the lands designated as their reserves.

The thorough knowledge of the Indians of California possessed by Mr. Wilson, and the great influence he has over them, were sources of great assistance to Mr. Beale in this negotiation. Mr. Wilson vouched to the Indians for the good intentions of the Government on the present occasion, and assured them that although previous failures had been made, all Mr. Beale's promises should now be fulfilled.

Mr. Beale was obliged to leave the Four Creeks without holding his contemplated Council with the Indians there, in consequence of business which required his immediate attention in San Francisco. We congratulate Mr. Beale, and are sure all our citizens will join us in the congratulations, upon the success which has thus far attended his labors.

[San Francisco *Alta California*, September 22, 1853.]

*

... It has become a question whether these unfortunate people [the California Indians] shall be exterminated as soon as possible, or remain in their present degraded, defenceless, and hopeless condition, or become the subject of judicious and just care on the part of the General Government, and be elevated in the scale of humanity to the position of a civilized and self-dependent people. The first proposition is too revolting to all sense of justice and common humanity to be entertained by a virtuous and Christian public; the second is too nearly allied to the first to be decided upon as a system of policy.... The third alternative is demanded by a consideration of national justice to the Indians, and a regard for the interest of the State....

The plan ... is simple, economical, and calculated to impart the greatest moral, intellectual and physical benefits to the Indians that they are capable of receiving.... The Superintendent purposes commencing his operations with the Indians in the southern part of the Tulare plains; the reservation to be located in the vicinity of Tejon. The tribes in that region, with some of whom Mr. Beale recently held an official "talk," have a natural taste for agricultural pursuits, which they practice now to some extent....

The advantages of this plan are obvious and great; indeed, it is impossible to devise any other that would so effectually protect the whites from the predatory incursions of the Indians, or shield the Indians against the injustice and oppression of the whites....

A system that is so simple, so practicable, and leading to results so beneficial to both races, and so honorable to the American name, will surely command the support and co-operation of the people of California, as well as of the General Government.

[Editorial, San Francisco *Alta California*, September 22, 1853.]

*

E. F. BEALE TO GEORGE W. MANYPENNY

San Francisco, September 30, 1853

In pursuance of the intention which I communicated to you in my letter of the 26th ultimo, I left Los Angeles on the 30th, and arrived at the Tejon pass on the 2d instant.

I found the Indians in that quarter quietly engaged in farming, but anxious to know the intentions of the government towards them. Mr. Edwards, whom I had employed as farming agent, had been unable to assure them of anything permanent in relation to their affairs. He had, however, with great tact, and with the assistance of Mr. Alexander Godey, by travelling from tribe to tribe and talking constantly with them, succeeded in preventing any outbreak, or disturbance in the San Joaquin valley. I immediately collected together the headmen and chiefs, and deputations from every quarter of the mountains and plains lying between the "Four Rivers" and that point, a distance of about one hundred and fifteen miles in length by about the same in breadth.

With these Indians I held council for two days, explaining to them the intentions of the government in relation to their future support. After long deliberation and much talk among the headmen and chiefs, they agreed to accept the terms I had offered them, which were as follows:

The government should commence with a system of farming and instruction, which would enable them in a few years to support themselves by the produce of their own labor.

That for this purpose the government would furnish them with seed of all kinds, and with provisions sufficient to enable them to live until the produce of their own labor should be sufficient to support them. I pointed out to them the impossibility of their remaining any longer a barrier to the rapid settlement of the State, and of the necessity which existed that they should leave their old homes in the mountains, and settle at some other point where the government would be able to watch over and protect them from the whites, as well as the whites from them. I pointed out to them, also, the difference between themselves and those who had embraced this new mode of life, as farmers, at the Tejon, and endeavored to make them sensible of the difference between a certain and reliable means of support by the produce of their own labor, and the exceedingly precarious one of dependence upon the spontaneous productions of the soil; and that even this mode of existence, precarious as it is, was becoming still more uncertain by the rapid increase of our white population. To all this I had no difficulty in bringing them to assent. A difficulty, however, arose here, which it was very hard to overcome. This was their disinclination to leave their old homes and hunting grounds and to settle so far away from them; and I found it utterly impossible to overcome this difficulty until I had promised them that the reserve selected for them should be somewhere in the vicinity of the place where that conference was held. On my promising this, they consented unanimously to my proposition; and I have no doubt that they are all, by this time, on the spot awaiting my return.

Before I determined, however, upon locating the reserve at that point, I called upon Lieutenants Stoneman, Parke, and Williamson, of the United States army, who had been surveying the country carefully with a view to the location of the proposed Atlantic and Pacific railroad, to know whether, in their opinion, there was any other point north as far as the Sacramento river where an Indian reservation containing the requisites of good land, wood, and water, and also sufficiently accessible to admit of the establishment of a military post, existed within their knowledge. The reply of these gentlemen, coinciding as it did with my own knowledge of the country, and with the views of Mr. Wilson, late Indian agent, on whose experience I placed great reliance, determined me in the selection of that point as one of the reservations authorized by the act of Congress. . . .

[*Report of the Commissioner of Indian Affairs*, 1853, pp. 469-72.]

*

B. D. WILSON TO E. F. BEALE

Los Angeles, October 4, 1853

I arrived here last night I found my family all well. I Sent for Andrew Sublette Early this morning he has been in and seen me about the contract of delivery of the grain at the Texon I have talked the matter over with A. and he thinks that he ought to have for the wheat 22cts. pr. bb, and 20 for the barley delivered at the Texon, the price seems high but I dont believe a man can make wages at lower prices I have parcially agreed with him at the above but I told him I would not consider the contract closed definitely until the Boat returned so I could hear your opinion on the prices he is willing for Young to be his partner & wishes for him to come down immediately Should Young and yourself think well of the arrangement it would be to Andrews & Youngs advantage to get in San Francisco the use of as much money at the start as would enable them to start here without borrowing as money here is worth at the lowest 5 pr ct pr month it will not be posible for them to buy Grain Enough here to Supply the contract at the texon consequently they will have to ship from San Francisco the greater portion especially the wheat. Wheat here is worth from 6 to 7 cents now & probably will raise in a short time now it may be that 100,000 lbs of wheat is more than you may want at the Texon reflect on it and should you think less would do advise me.

I hope you will be here soon the Indians are very anxious to see you there was a large delegation from red River (the Colorado) the other day but left before I got home but I believe intend to return in a short time I feel certain you should come to this quiet place in order that you might recover from the perplixities of San Francisco. I know that politicians and other hum-bugs have nearly Distracted you ere this I send Fred the box of Grapes and a box of pears though I have no doubt but he will divide with you all. Fred must divide with Mr. Sanders & Branham and I will send him another box in a few days.

I have been quite unwell since my departure from San Francisco and I have a light fever on me at this time so if this letter is not very interesting I hope you will Excuse it.

[Draft, Wilson Papers, Huntington Library.]

*

B. D. WILSON TO CAVE J. COUTS

Los Angeles, October 6, 1853

Sir. Yours bearing date on the 2nd present has been duly rcd. As I am sick and not able to write you lengthly I will merely say to you that I have just returnd from the north where I have been on an Indian tour with Mr. Beale the Suppnt. I left him (Mr. B.) in San Francisco he told me he would be here by the 15 Inst. without fail and then we would take a travel through the Southern Indians and make arrangements to Settle the Indians permanently. So please let things remain as they are until Mr. Beale arrives then I have no doubt but you will have us at your place

[Wilson Papers, Huntington Library.]

*

E. F. BEALE TO B. D. WILSON

[*San Francisco*] *October* 15, 1853

You will please contract for the delivery, on the Indian Reservation, at the Texon, of five hundred head of cattle.

[Wilson Papers, Huntington Library.]

*

E. F. BEALE TO B. D. WILSON

San Francisco, October 17, 1853

With the bearer you will receive Seven Indians. I am sending them to the reservation on the Tejon & wish you to forward them by the first train which leaves with Andrew Sublettes wheat.

Please be attentive to Mr. Blackstone who accompanies them & get them off as soon as possible.

[Wilson Papers, Huntington Library.]

*

INDIANS FOR THE RESERVE

A deputation of young men from the tribes about Grass Valley arrived on Saturday evening by the Sacramento boat. They will leave for Los Angeles in the first boat and go thence to the reserve set apart for them. They will remain upon the reserve a short time, travel over a considerable portion of it, and then come back to report to their tribes. If their report be favorable, it is probable that all the tribes will move down to the reservation this spring. The Indians are distrustful but it is hoped that they will have confidence in Lieut. Beale, who has taken hold of the duties of his office with a proper energy and feeling for the unfortunate Indians. Nearly all the whites living near the Indians are anxious for their removal, except a few selfish traders who profit by the ignorance and vices of the red men.

[San Francisco *Alta California*, October 17, 1853.]

*

Los Angeles, October 25, 1853

We arrived safely in the *Los Angeles* after stopping at all the intermediate ports, if ports they can be called, for not a point which I saw between San Francisco and San Pedro can have a safe harbor, and consequently they cannot be places of much importance in a commercial view. The climate of this place is delightful, and at some day Los Angeles will be a favorite resort for invalids. The white-washed adobe walls have a very rude appearance, but the march of improvements is steady and certain....

That indefatigable officer, Lieut. Beale, is already moving in his department. A deputation of young Indians from Nevada county, arrived here last Sunday in charge of Capt. Nathaniel Blackstone, destined for their new home at Tejon Pass. The Indians in this vicinity are very degraded, and murders are of frequent occurrence among them. A large portion of their sins lies at the door of those traders who seek an unholy profit by selling intoxicating liquors to the poor red man. Lieut. Beale is expected to be here shortly, and it is hoped he will try, and succeed, to put a stop to this wicked traffic.   POTOMAC

[San Francisco *Alta California*, November 1, 1853.]

*

B. D. WILSON TO E. F. BEALE

Los Angeles, November 8, 1853

In accordance with your order bearing date of 16 last month I have made arrangements with Messrs. Sanford & Reed to deliver 200 head of large beef Cattle at the Tejon Reserve for which I have agreed to pay Sixty dollars per head this being the best arrangement I could make for large cattle such as they are to deliver. Mr. Reed says there may be a few over 200, but I have told him I had no doubt you would take them.

Hoping the above will prove satisfactory....

[Signed copy, Wilson Papers, Huntington Library.]

*

H. B. EDWARDS TO B. D. WILSON

Los Angeles, November 15, 1853

When I saw you this morning I neglected to mention that Mr. Beale had requested Godey to drive up some goats, which he purchased from you when in Los Angeles. You will, of course, know the number. I know nothing about the transaction.

Mr. Beale will settle with you for them when he comes down.

[Wilson Papers, Huntington Library.]

*

Lt. Beale is still at the Tejon. It will be seen by an advertisement in another place, that emigrants and travellers may not make the Tejon a point at which to procure supplies of provisions, etc. The supplies lodged at that place are intended for government uses and not for the travelling public. This intelligence may be of importance to persons expecting to replenish their stock of provisions on the road.

[Los Angeles *Star*, December 3, 1853.]

*

FROM THE COLORADO

Maj. Harvey, Special Indian Agent, who went to the Colorado about a month since, for the purpose of reporting upon the number and condition of the Indians in that region and selecting a site for a Reserve, returned to town this week. He has selected a reserve to the north of the Fort, and has made preparations for erecting a house for his own use. Major H. estimates the number of Yumas who will be brought under his supervision, at from 6000 to 7000; and it is probable that the Mohaves will be added to that number. At present every thing is quiet, though every day shows the necessity of convincing these Indians of the power and unity of our government.

[Los Angeles *Star*, December 3, 1853.]

*

INDIAN ARRESTS

It has long been a practice with the Indians of this city, to get drunk on Saturday night. Their ambition seems to be to earn sufficient money, through the week, to treat themselves handsomely at the close of it. In this they only follow the white examples; and like white men they are often noisy about the streets.

It has also been a practice, with the City Marshal and his associates, to spend the Sabbath in arresting and imprisoning Indians supposed to be drunk, until Monday morning, when they are taken before the Mayor and discharged on paying a bill of two dollars and a half each, one dollar of which is the fee of the Marshal. Sometimes of a Monday morn we have seen the Marshal marching in procession with twenty or twenty five of these poor people; and truly, it is a brave sight.

Now we have no heart to do the Marshal the slightest prejudice, but this leading off of Indians and locking them up at night, for the purpose of taking away their paltry dollars, seems to us a questionable act; especially as they are seldom quarrelsome; and, more especially, as, unlike some white men whom the Marshal is too discreet to arrest; they do not, when drunk, brandish knives and pistols through the streets, threatening the safety of quiet citizens. We shall rejoice if the decision of Judge Hayes, declaring the practice unlawful, has the effect to put a wholesome check upon it; for there are other subjects, far more worthy the attention of the Marshal, upon whom he can exercise the duties of his office.

[Los Angeles *Star*, December 3, 1853.]

*

INDIAN PUNISHMENT

Last Sunday week at the mission of San Gabriel, the Indians got drunk and some of them quarrelled. One of them, named Jose, retired to the bushes where he lay till night,when he rose up,took an axe and smote one Salvador on the head,so that he died the following Thursday.The Indians after consultation, resolved that they would punish the murderer according to law; and they hung him by the neck until he was dead.

[Los Angeles *Star*, December 3, 1853.]

*

E. F. BEALE TO B. D. WILSON

Tejon, January 9, 1854

In the party of Lieut. Williamson Top. Eng. U. S. Army there was a blacksmith, and should you be able to find him I wish you would employ him for me. I am paying One hundred and twenty five dollars pr. month, but should you not be able to hire him at that price, offer him one hundred and fifty as he is a good workman and I need his services at this Post, he can come out with Thompson's pack train. If you can not get him I do not wish any other

[Wilson Papers, Huntington Library.]

*

E. F. BEALE TO GEORGE W. MANYPENNY

Tejon, February 8, 1854

Being about to return to San Francisco on official business, I
have the honor to report progress at this place. Since my last,
I have completed our wheat-field, and the whole two thousand acres is now covered with the coming crop, and presents
a beautiful prospect of the plenty which will reward our labor when we shall have gathered its grain. I am now planting
barley, of which I shall sow five hundred acres; after which,
a hundred and fifty acres of corn will complete the heavy part
of my work for this season.

This, you will remember, is exclusive of the separate portion which I plant for each tribe, and which, I informed you,
is to be placed at their entire disposal, while the large crops
I have mentioned will be served out in regular and sufficient
rations.

It is impossible to do justice to the docility and energy
which these poor people possess. They work not only without murmur or complaint, but with the most cheerful alac-
rity; and as the fruits of their labor begin to show themselves
in the immense field, now covered with its verdant promise
of future plenty, they look at it in amazement, and with delight.

You must perceive in the fact that I have punished a few
lazy ones with proper but not severe correction, a proof of the
discipline which is here maintained by a moral force which is
exerted over their minds by the majority, and that this influence could and would never have been exerted but for the
confidence they feel in what I have told them, that all this
work is to benefit themselves, and not the government.This,
then, is the first great point gained, viz. An established confidence in their own minds that the government really desires

their good, and not to exterminate them, as malicious and reckless white men have informed them.

If this had not been done, you will perceive it would be impossible for me to control, with the dozen white employes I have here, some twenty-five hundred Indians. So perfect is the discipline, that not even one of them ever leaves his work for a single day without permission, or returns without reporting his arrival.

You must not suppose I have merely brought the ploughs here, and the grain and all the stores which my returns show, and given them to the Indians, telling them to go to work. On the contrary, I have toiled from an hour before daylight until dark with the few hired white men I have employed, and showed them how to manage the instruments put into their hands. It has been a labor of excessive toil, only compensated by the aptitude of the scholars, and cheered by the most pre-eminent success. I have endeavored to transplant here a system and regularity, acquired by eighteen years' experience in the strict school of naval discipline; and I have not been unsuccessful, as the results show. My Indians are divided into different working parties. Those who plough and harrow, seventy-five in number, go to the field after harnessing, in regular order; those who ditch have their work laid out—each one so much, according to the nature of the soil; and so on through every department of work which happens at the time to be necessary. Their dinner meals are cooked and eaten in the field; breakfast and supper at the village. Their tasks are never made laborious, so that an hour before sundown their work is always finished.

I have clothed them coarsely, but comfortably, and on Sunday (work having ceased on Saturday at noon) they seem as happy as it is possible to conceive. To that day I have en-

couraged them to look as one of pleasure, and for this purpose
have instituted among them our own games, in which I have
requested and encouraged my white employes to take part;
so that on every Sunday we have sometimes two or three hundred playing at bandy and ball with those who during the
week are their overseers and instructors in manual labor.

In fact, so happy are my people, that that which I never
thought possible has come to pass, and my feelings for this
poor race, which at first were merely those of compassion, are
rapidly changing into a deep interest in their welfare, and in
many instances to a personal attachment.

I have no military force here, and require none; my door
has neither been locked nor barred night or day, and yet my
feeling of security is as great as though I were surrounded by
an armed guard.

Among other labors executed here, I have by a ditch six
feet in width by eight in depth, and running for a distance of
nine miles, connected two streams and thrown them completely around the immense field in which I have sown my
grain, putting the certainty of my crops beyond peradven-
ture, by giving me the power to irrigate the entire field with
comparatively little labor.

On the first of next May I shall further elaborate my system, by choosing six among the chiefs most intelligent, and
forming them, with myself to preside, into a council to decide
upon certain laws for our interior government, and also on
what shall be done with our surplus produce, which must be
very great. This council will meet on the first of every month
to discuss matters of interest to our reserve, to look constantly
to our future welfare and prospects, as well as to fix appropri-
ate punishments and settle whatever may need arrangement
among us. Thus, by degrees, I hope to raise these people to

believe that God has not created them to live and die as the wolves and beasts of their mountains. Already some faint and indistinct notion that such may be the case appears to have struck their sight; but as yet it is vague and distant, like the first uncertain glimpse of a distant light-house. Constantly, they say to me, "We have been asleep a long time. We are just beginning to awake, but our eyes are not yet wide open."

The extending influence of this policy is already felt. But a few days since, the chief who controls almost the entire race of valley Indians, and hitherto considered as beyond reclaiming, visited me with some fifty of his tribe. He came to stay a day; he remained a fortnight. When he left me he said, "I came here to laugh at your work, and to take back some of my people who were with you. I go away with peace in my heart; and if not another Indian of the valley comes, I will make my home with you. In two months I shall return with my people." Should this promise be kept, he will bring with him not less than five thousand Indians; and these, sir, will have been removed without force and without expense, and, above all, without entailing on our government the bitter disgrace of punishing Indians because they do not willingly abandon the homes of their childhood and the graves of their sires.

Their ingenuity is carried into every branch of manufacture. I have seen one of them, a lame boy, carefully unravel a piece of worsted saddle-girth, and in three months after, with instruments made by his own hands, produce the garters I enclose you. They were intended as a present to myself, and to be used to tie the leather leggins necessary here to protect the limbs in riding through a thorny undergrowth in hunting game. Much as I value them, I cheerfully resign the gift to you, as a proof of what they are capable. I have watched this boy day after day with patient toil improving his imperfect implements, and working until he has produced that which I send you. It may be considered by the department a small matter, but with me it has enlarged significance; and I repeat that such ingenuity, (for this is but one instance in many I could mention,) and such constancy in labor, deserve and should receive the fostering care of a government which possesses in its treasury so many unappropriated millions.

[*Report of the Commissioner of Indian Affairs*, 1854, pp. 506-508.]

*

H. B. EDWARDS TO B. D. WILSON

San Francisco, March 18, 1854

Your letter enclosing Thompson's receipt, has been received, and I feel much indebted for the trouble you have had in the matter.

I don't consider it at all necessary to purchase any more wheat, if Bishop has already finished sowing it, as there is probably a sufficient quantity there now to last until the crop comes on, if used sparingly. If, however, Thompson has purchased, it makes no difference.

The order from Alexander & Baning was presented and promptly paid.

I will send by Adams & Co's Express, to your order, a draft for two thousand dollars which you will please hand to Thompson. I expect to go down by the next Steamer, by which time I hope the work will be finished. It is impossible for me to leave San Francisco for any length of time, otherwise I would go in the "Fremont" today. I hope the present draft will be sufficient to keep things straight until I can get down myself.

San francisco is totally devoid of news. Politicians are all busy with the Senatorial question, and merchants working hard to keep their heads above water, in which several have failed to succeed.

Present my kindist regards to Mrs. Wilson and the children, & believe me.

P. S. I am sorry to trouble you again about this business, but I was uncertain where Thompson would be, and determined to impose again upon your good nature, with a promise to sin no more hereafter.

[Wilson Papers, Huntington Library.]

*

SAMUEL R. DUMMER TO B. D. WILSON

Tejon, April 4, 1854

I have been requested by Mr. Edwards to forward to you for him a statement of the number of lbs. of Wheat and Barley received here from Mr. James Thompson, and enclosed I have sent you the same which you will please forward to him.

I wish you would let me have a few strawberry plants for Mrs. Beale's garden: I have given directions to White Elliott that in case you can spare any to take care of them without giving you any trouble.

My sheep and their *descendants* are doing well; I have reserved 80 Rams as these (Chihuahua) sheep are much larger than the ordinary California breeds;—these rams are now four months old and in a few months will be fit for breeding purposes, and should you think proper to give me, say four or five hundred ewes I will put in the 80 rams and take care of the ewes and their increase for any length of time you may designate for half their increase.

Our crops begin to look well, and every thing connected with the Reservation is going on properly and with spirit. Remember me to Mrs. Wilson and your children

[Wilson Papers, Huntington Library.]

*

SAMUEL R. DUMMER TO H. B. EDWARDS

Tejon, April 4, 1854

With this I send you the amount of Wheat and Barley received at this Post up to this date, which is, Ninety two thousand eight hundred and eighty five lbs. of Wheat, and ninety five thousand seven hundred and fifty five lbs. of Barley.

Mr. Bishop has directed me to say to you that we will need the balance of the Wheat for the subsistence of the Indians and he thinks you had better purchase it at once and forward it here. Mr. B. and all hands send their respects to you.

ENDORSEMENT BY B. D. WILSON

Los Angeles, April 12, 1854

Mr. Thompson requested me to say to you that if you wished to send the grain to San Pedro that he would sent it out to the Texon at once he says you should send good bags for to pack the grain in.

P. S. Godey has not come yet. I hear he is on the road.

[Wilson Papers, Huntington Library.]

*

H. B. EDWARDS TO B. D. WILSON

San Francisco, April 26, 1854

I send by the Steamer "Southerner" ten thousand (10000) of wheat the quantity I believe to be deficient in order to make up the one hundred thousand pounds.

Please ask Thompson to send me by the return of this Steamer the receipts from the Texon, for the barley and wheat for which I settled with him, viz: one hundred thousand pounds of the former and ninety thousand of the latter. It is necessary I should have them.

I also send per Adams Co. to your order, one thousand (1000) dollars, five hundred of which you will please forward

to Bishop by the first opportunity, and the remainder retain
in your possession subject to his order, or give such portion
of it to Godey as may be necessary to defray any Expenses he
may incur in carrying out Mr. Beale's orders.

You will also receive some rose cuttings, which were given
to me by a friend of mine here. He says, however, that he has
but little idea they will grow, the season now being too far advanced to plant such things. He has promised to let me know
when the proper time arrives, and then give me a greater variety which I will place at Mrs.Wilson's disposal.

The receipt from Adams Co. for that money you will find
enclosed, as well as some letters which you will oblige me by
forwarding to the Texon, when an opportunity offers.

Present my kindest regards to Mrs. Wilson and believe me,
[Wilson Papers, Huntington Library.]

*

AFRIVAL OF COL. NORRIS

Col. Norris arrived in town this week from the desert by way
of Turner's Pass, having completed his contract for surveying the government lands. He brings us favorable intelligence
from the Tejon....

At the Tejon, after a month of very warm and dry weather,
a rain, accompanied with thunder, lightening, hail and snow,
on the mountains, and severe cold, had put a very improving
face upon all things. The crops look well, and promise great
abundance.

There are some twelve hundred Indians at the reservation.
The Colonel reports every thing well and prosperous, and
gives much praise to Lieutenant Beale and his employees for
their energy and perseverance in their labors.
[Los Angeles *Star*, May 6, 1854.]

*

CAVE J. COUTS TO B. D. WILSON

Guajomito, May 7, 1854

Manuelito, Captain of the San Luis Rey Indians, has called to request a letter to you, asking for the delivery of one of his Indians (named Mateo) who run away from here about six weeks since and is now in San Gabriel—said to be with a Don George, (an American) who promised to let Manuelito have him in case pursuit was made.

Mateo was pursued as far as San Juan, when they heard of his passing Los Angeles, and returned. Manuelito was willing to let him alone as he had left here; but it appears that the Indians in the mountains have held a council and requested their Captain to send after him.

He, Mateo, is lame in one leg, a very intelligent indian (can read & write), and their charges against him are for stealing & murder (as a *witch* or echisero). He has been pardoned by these Indians seven times, and they appear very anxious for you to aid them in getting him.

P. S. You have probably noticed a card published in the *Star*, purporting to be from the citizens of Sta. Ysabel, respecting the removal of *Tomas*, and appointment of *Lazzaro* over the Dieguinos Indians.

1′ Lazarro was not appointed. *Panto*, at the request of the rancheros (except Sta.Ysabel) was appointed in place of Tomas, for various reasons.

2° I have been able to find *no one* who knows more than two or three of the names to the paper. They may be *strangers* in the employ of the quartermaster (Br. Maj. Justin McKinstry).

3d The whole matter resulted from a *personal* matter, between a notorious *public money handler*, called *Br. Maj. Justin McKinstry* a qm. in San Diego, & myself, previous to my leaving the army—when he proved himself a *liar, slander,* & *coward,* & was so *proclaimed.*

4' This notorious public money handler, calls himself the owner of Sta. Ysabel.

[Wilson Papers, Huntington Library.]

*

CAVE J. COUTS TO B. D. WILSON

[*Guajomito*] *May* 7, 1854

There has been a hard attempt made by the rascal alluded to, to have me removed thinking that his position as a Qur. master in the *U. S. Army*, would be sufficient with *Beale* to Crush any humble Citizen.

I only sought the appt. of the *San Luis Indians*, and never meddled with the Dieguinos until the most prominent Rancherros in their midst Call twice, *requesting the removal of Tomas & appt. of Panto.*

The publications that you may see on the subject, be assured are from him (Br. Maj. McKinstry) or his *hired bullies*.

Beale arrived in San Diego a short time since, and, as I understand, was prevailed upon by the rascal to reappoint old Tomas. I made as brief a statement of the facts to him as I could, advising him that Tomas could not act as Capt. of the Indians so long as I remained the Sub-Agent—any orders that he might wish, to communicate to the Inds. thro' me would be promptly attended to. The matter, I judge, will shortly be maad up by Beale dispensing with my services.

My only object, as you know, was to regulate the San Luis Indians. They are well regulated, and if it was not for this man's attempt to have me relieved, would now, or probably sooner, have asked to be relieved.

If you should see Beale shortly, please suggest that he see a few of the Citizens of this county (not quarter masters employees) and ascertain from them the Course of the Sub. Indn. agent.

[Wilson Papers, Huntington Library.]

*

CAVE J. COUTS TO B. D. WILSON

Guajomito, June 5, 1854

The enclosed letter to Beale, I leave open that you may see it. I care not a straw for his removing me; but am a little annoyed at his sending me word that he removes me on account of an old difficulty of five years standing with the notorious *handler of public funds*. What did this have to do with *Indian affairs?*

From the acquaintance&knowledge I have of Beale,thought him above medling in any such operations.

If you have any influence with Beale, try and get some *Citizen* of the county appointed in place of Capt. Burton.

On account of the sparce population of this county, the *army* has been riding it, *rough shod*, since the formation of the state constitution. This I shall kick against as long as I have fingers & toes.

N. B. I shall continue to act as sub agent until *officially informed* or until Capt. Burton, or some one else, shows me that they have the appointment, *officially*.

[Wilson Papers, Huntington Library.]

*

THE TEJON RESERVATION—SUPERINTENDENT BEALE

The peculiar adaptation of the Tejon to its present uses cannot but be acknowledged by every one who will visit it. It lies in a corner of the world, far away from civilization, and defying the approach of settlements on any side. It is off from the line of travel, and the only resources of its people are in the soil and wild game. South and East it is bounded by almost impassable mountains; on the North is a strip of arid desert, extending to the Tules; on its extreme West passes the wagon trail from the Canada de las Uvas. The Tejon Pass, which is in the extreme east corner, is only a single trail, through a narrow defile, broken by precipitous and difficult hills. It is

so cut off from the world that travellers must go out of their
way to approach it. It is so far from markets, and so difficult
of access, that it could be of little value for any other purpose,
except it be as a grazing rancho. It is about twenty miles across
the head of the valley, and the Reservation embraces 50,000
acres. The soil is rich, and abundantly supplied with water
and timber. Indeed, one can have little idea of its capacities,
without close examination. We rode a distance of probably
twenty-five miles around its borders. Little green vallies extend into the Sierras, supplied with clear spring water, and
belts of oak timber. In these vallies are located the *rancherias*,
out of sight of the general observer, where the Indians cultivate their acres, and take as much pride in keeping them clean
and free from weeds as any other class of farmers. All classes
work, from the oldest to the youngest. Juan Viejo claimed ex-
emption on account of being Chief; but when told it was necessary for the old men to set the example of industry to the
young, he replied, "It is good," and went cheerfully to the field.

Considering the short time since Lieutenant Beale arrived
at the Tejon, and the obstacles he has overcome, the amount
of labor performed is almost miraculous. At first the Indians
were shy and awkward—fearful that tricks were about to be
practiced on them, as had been done by former Indian Agents.
All the implements had to be transported over an almost impassable road. Yet in spite of these difficulties, the Tejon, once
a barren waste, roamed over by bear and deer and antelopes,
and a few poor Indians, has become a blooming field and garden. All these results have been produced since the first day
of November last, when the first ground was broken by the
plow. Previous to this the Indians resident had raised small
crops of corn and melons, by stirring up the earth, and drop-
ping the seed to take care of itself; but their crops were never

sufficient; and in seasons of drought, they lived upon roots, nuts, venison, and fish taken from the lake. The mountains abound in bears and deer, and the plains are alive with antelope....

It is to be hoped that the Government may not be so short-sighted nor so unwise, as to withhold the small amount of money necessary to complete the plan of colonization; and that the office of Superintendent may never be put into the political market, thus jeopardizing the redemption of the Indians from the temptations of the white man and from barbarism. The Superintendent should live among them; understand their habits; and show them, by the interest he takes in their labors that the Government is in earnest in its efforts to redeem and protect them. The work is but just begun; yet the results are marvellous. And these results are attributable to the confidence which the Indians feel in the men who direct their labors, and in their constant presence with them.

Mr. Beale is a man of untiring energy, and is entirely and unselfishly devoted to the work. Let him have a fair trial, and he will make the miserable wild Indians of California the happiest people in the State. He is a young man, and, of course, is ambitious; but his ambition lies in a road which few have the capacity or taste to travel, and therefore, though he may be closely watched, there are none who ought to envy him his success. In the revolutions of party and the desire to reward favorites, he may be replaced. For the good cause in which he is engaged, and for the sake of degraded humanity, we hope the day of his displacement is far off. But should the evil time come, when his office shall descent into the vortex of politics, we trust the Government will insist that his successor be fitted for the post, that he reside upon the Reservations and follow out the system already so auspiciously commenced and which is admirably suited to the character and associations of the California Indians.

[Los Angeles *Star*, June 24, 1854.]

*

F. E. KERLIN TO B. D. WILSON

Tejon, July 16, 1854

I send the Indian boy down with letters, and wish him to wait until some news comes from San Francisco.

The Indians, are very much displeased at the idea of Mr. Beale leaving them, and I think they will give "Uncle Sam," a great deal of trouble if some steps are not taken with them. Dummer wishes me to give his kind regards to yourself and Mrs. Wilson.

Bishop left here yesterday to bring back one hundred Indians, who left for Owens Lake on the 14th Inst.

With many regards to Mrs. Wilson

Please request Harry or Mr. Sanford to settle the boys stable, and board bill, & give him bustamente, for the road.

[Wilson Papers, Huntington Library.]

*

THOMAS J. HENLEY, *Superintendent of Indian Affairs in California*, TO GEORGE W. MANYPENNY

San Francisco, August 28, 1854

Since entering upon my official duties on the 26th ultimo, in accordance with my instructions of June 2, 1854, I have visited the Indian reservation at Tejon, (the only reservation at which, as yet, any Indians have been collected,) and have taken possession and supervision of the public property, schedules of which will accompany my report at the expiration of the quarter.

I could not ascertain the precise number of Indians belonging to the Tejon reservation, as many of them were in the mountains, upon an excursion which a portion usually take at this season of the year, to collect grass-seeds and berries which they find there in great abundance, and of which they are very fond. I fix the number, however, according to the best information I could obtain, at severn hundred, who acknowledge the authority of seventeen chiefs. These Indians many of them speak the Spanish language, having learned it during their intercourse with the Mexicans, and at the "Catholic Missions," where some of them have been previously employed, and where they acquired some knowledge of agriculture previous to the settlement of California by the people of the United States.

The plan of subsisting the Indians by their own labor in the cultivation of the soil, I presume was suggested by the success which has attended the efforts of the Catholic priests in applying Indian labor to the erection of the mission buildings, and to the cultivation of their vineyards and grounds. . . .

The grand features of the [reservation] plan can, with proper and judicious management, be made partially if not entirely successful. The Indians in the southern and central portions of the State are willing to labor, and many are anxious to avail themselves of the privilege of settling upon the reservations. I do not, therefore, hesitate to give it as my opinion that the plan of removing them to suitable reservations, requiring them to labor, and issuing to them only such articles of food and clothing from time to time as will supply their immediate wants, is the only method that can be adopted calculated to do permanent good to the Indians in California. To distribute to them beef, blankets, or clothing, in their present locations, would result in more injury than in causing them to become indolent, and to cease effort to provide the necessary support for themselves. To remove them beyond the limits of the State, or into the high mountain region, without providing for their support, would be worse and more cruel than immediate extermination. The Indians upon the west, unlike those east of the Rocky mountains, have never lived by the chase. Their support has been chiefly derived from the fish of our numerous streams, the acorns and grass-seeds of our valleys, and the roots and berries of the mountains. By the encroachment of the white man they have been driven from their habitations, and their means of living entirely cut off. There seems then to be no alternative which humanity would sanction but to provide them with the necessary tools and implements, and suitable instruction to enable them to obtain a support by their own labor on your lands reserved for that purpose.

The reservation at the Tejon, considering its interior location, difficulty of access, and the delays and trouble which always attend new enterprises, has probably been conducted with considerable energy, and so far as I could judge, the labor has been well performed. The wheat crop is a good one, and may be considered as entirely successful. The barley, having been sown late, was not a full crop. The corn suffered from drought, was not irrigated, and was also deficient in quantity. The raising of vegetables has been almost entirely neglected. The land now in cultivation, about fifteen hundred acres, is enclosed by a ditch; but it is not adequate to the protection of the crop, and some portion of it has this year been destroyed by the stock. There are upon the reservation one old adobe building used as a residence for the persons employed upon the farm, and one new adobe intended for the residence of the superintendent. There are also a sufficient number of corrals for taking care of the stock.

The Indians are not as yet provided with any houses, and

are living in such habitations as they are accustomed to in their wild state....

The Indians, on my arrival at the reservation, were quite anxious to learn if any change had taken place in the intention of the government towards them; and, on assembling in council, it appeared that they had decided objection to the Indian interpreter, and also to the two men in whose charge they had been placed by my predecessor. This objection being removed, I met with no other difficulty; and after several conversations, I left them well satisfied and contented, with an unqualified promise to obey all the orders of those in whose charge I left them. The chiefs, at their own request, have been permitted to exercise police authority over their respective tribes, and are held responsible for the proper quota of labor from each tribe. The labor is divided among the chiefs, according to the number in each tribe; the making of adobes to one, laying them in the building to a second, threshing wheat, &c., to a third, hauling grain from the field to a fourth, &c., &c. In this way the work progresses in perfect order, and all seem pleased at their participation in it.

The location of the reservation is, in my judgment, a good one—the best that could have been made. The soil is good, and well adapted to the cultivation of such products as are necessary for Indian subsistence. There is an abundance of oak timber at a convenient distance, and plenty of red-wood and pine in the mountains, at accessible points within fifteen miles. The lake within the limits of the reservation affords an abundant supply of fish of a good quality. Game is plenty, and a hunter, at ordinary wages, will furnish meat as cheaply as the beef that is now issued to the Indians. It is remote from the present settlements of our citizens, and will not, I think, for a long time to come, be a barrier even to the progressive and

laudable spirit of our people in the settlement of new and remote portions of our Territory.

If the Indians are to be allowed any resting-place within
the limits of the State, no attention, in my opinion, ought to
be given to any clamor that might be raised against this location, as tending to embarrass the settlement and prosperity
of the State....

The above-named tribes [the Kern River Indians, Posa
Creek Indians, Tulare River Indians, the Four Creeks, the
Y-Mithes, and Cowiahs, the King River, the San Joaquin,
and the Fresno River Indians], numbering about three thousand souls, reside at an average distance of two hundred miles
from the Tejon reservation. Their removal will not be expensive, and can be accomplished as speedily as the advances of
the settlements, the interests of the government, or humanity
to the Indians, will require.

The crops which will be planted this winter will in all probability be abundant for the support of those referred to, and
all the other tribes within reach of the reservation; and in the
course of next year a large number may easily be added to
those now enjoying the benefits of the reservation....

[*Report of the Commissioner of Indian Affairs*, 1854, pp. 508-13.]

*

[ALONZO RIDLEY] TO THOMAS J. HENLEY

Sebastian Military Reserve, September 22, 1854

... In the spring of 1850, an American named French settled
in this valley, and built one of the adobe houses now in use
on the reservation. His business was taking care of stock on
shares; but in 1851, on account of Indian disturbances at the
Four Creeks, and other outbreaks, he left the place. In May,
1852, Alonzo Ridley and David McKenzie came here for the
purpose of trading with the Indians. After trading a short

time, they left for about two months, and returning, took up their permanent residence. At the time of their first visit, and when they commenced their settlement, there were about three hundred Indians living here. They were called the Tejon Indians, and belonged to this valley. Their customs were, feasting and travelling a great deal, *though they had then corn and wheat fields the same as at the present*, except as regards quantity. They were very peaceable, and never committed any depredations on the whites. They were very improvident, and their liberality was unbounded. The mountain Indians, those in the immediate vicinity of the valley, from intermarriage with the Tejon Indians, have become one family. Many of them are what are called Mission Indians, having lived on the Spanish missions in time gone by. Some of them speak the Spanish language very well, and their conversation with the whites is held in this language. From what was taught them at the missions, they were enabled to plant and raise grain before the Americans came among them. When the old Spanish missions were secularized, these Indians were thrown back upon their former resources, though with the advantage of some knowledge of agriculture. On the opening of this reservation, this knowledge was practically displayed.

During the first year of the residence of Messrs. Ridley and McKenzie, the Indians were continually talking about the Americans, and expecting the agents and presents from our government so lavishly promised by Colonel Barbour in 1851. They had heard, also, that their treaties had not been ratified by our government, and grew discontented. Numerous tales were in circulation among them to the effect that the Americans intended killing them all, and for that reason they were anxious to commence killing first. The position of the Americans, at times, was by no means pleasant.

Mr. Beale, the former superintendent of Indian affairs, first visited the valley in August or September, 1853, one year since, for the purpose of selecting a reservation for the Indians. At that time, the number of Indians actually residing here was about three hundred and fifty. When he had determined on making this a reservation, he held a council with the Indians for that purpose, and his intentions were well received. Active operations were commenced about November. During the month, about twenty Indians from the Frezo [the Fresno] were brought in; they remained about one month, when they stole and ran away with eight horses on the reserve. From the Sacramento, or the north, seven were brought in under charge of a Mr. Storm. They also left in a short time, with the exception of a little boy named Lelo, now with Mr. Beale. From the Four Creeks there never have been over five or six at one time, and they did not remain. In the first six months on the reserve, the number of the Indians was increased to about six hundred, embracing all the Tejon tribes, and the tribes with which they were connected, who really belonged here, (with the exception of Juan's tribe of Lake Indians, numbering twenty-four men and their families,) and a few from the San Joaquin, Joaquin's tribe of twenty men from Kern river; which last were *sent off* by Mr. Beale's overseer, on hearing of Mr. Beale's removal. So that the Indians who have been actual residents, and now remain here, with the exception of Juan's and Joaquin's tribes, are none others but those actually belonging to this valley. According to all the information I can give on the subject, eight hundred Indians, great and small, old and young, is the highest number I have heard estimated, or can be proven to have been here *at any one time* since the commencement of the reserve.

[*Report of the Commissioner of Indian Affairs*, 1854, pp. 514-15.]

*

E. F. BEALE TO B. D. WILSON

San Francisco, October 14, 1854

This will introduce my friend Mr. J. Ross Brown[e], for whom I bespeak your cordial reception at Los Angeles.

I beg you will render him every assistance in your power, and endeavor to make his visit to your city agreeable.

Mr. Brown may require information on a variety of subjects and I have referred him to you as one whose position has placed it in his power to afford him all that he requires.

[Wilson Papers, Huntington Library.]

*

F. E. KERLIN TO B. D. WILSON

Washington, D. C., March 7, 1855

I am very happy to inform you that all our accounts have passed, and after all the attempts to injure Mr. Beales reputation they have been unable to justify any of the slanderous assertions put forward. I had intended writing to you before, this winter, but both Mr. Beale and myself were under the impression that you would be home, or rather in this country, before a letter could reach you, and you must blame yourself, for our not writing. I have been endeavoring to get your accounts up, and examined for some time and I think that in a week I will be able to effect a settlement for you; they are bound to pass, if anything will,—at any rate I will not leave anything undone to get them done at once: for although it is a matter of no importance pecuniarily to you, it will be no doubt more agreeable to have them all closed. Grayson the Clerk who will examine them is a clever person, and has promised me to go to work on them in a day or two.

Mr. Beale desires me to remember him most kindly to Mrs. W. & yourself. . . .

I hear that the Tejon is going to the dogs, as fast as negligence will let it. I am sorry for the Indians, but it is no more than was to be expected from that rotten politician Henley—who is the most contemptible fellow in California....

How is old Dummer getting on? I understand he has left the employ of Henley. Remember me to him when you see him....

[Wilson Papers, Huntington Library.]

*

LOS ANGELES SENATOR

We learn from Los Angeles, that the people of that county, native Californian and American, have united in urging Mr. Benj. D. Wilson to become a candidate for the State Senate, and that, after strong solicitation, he has consented. It is only when the people become sick and tired of office-seeking politicians, and demand to be represented by A MAN, that such men as Mr. Wilson are found in legislative bodies. To them office is no honor; on the contrary, they bestow respectability and honor upon the offices they are called upon to fill. Mr. Wilson has resided in the state about fifteen years, and is [so] thoroughly acquainted with the wants of the people, that he needs must become a useful member of the Legislature. Honest and fearless, he will be perfectly independent of all cliques and factions—a Senator that not only his own immediate constituents, but the people of the whole State, may be proud of.

[San Francisco *Alta California*, July 30, 1855.]

*

E. F. BEALE TO B. D. WILSON

San Francisco, August 29, 1855

I had hoped to hear from you by the last two Steamers but have been disappointed. I suppose you have been busy electioneering, and I sincerely hope successfully so.

From the last reports your election seems very certain,

though in such slippery matters as politics nothing is certain. Do let us hear from you soon, as we are all anxious to know how you get on....

Lewis tells me he has sent you Col: Bentons *last letter*. I *do not wish* it published in your papers for two reasons. I understand an investigation of Indian affairs in your district has been ordered, and to publish the letter of Col Benton would look like an attempt to prejudice Col: Henley, and I fear he has quite enough to answer for without that. So don't let it be republished in your papers....

[Wilson Papers, Huntington Library.]

＊

LOS ANGELES SENATOR

Benj. D. Wilson, Independent Whig, is elected to the Senate from the district composed of Los Angeles, San Bernardino and San Diego. Although the Democratic ticket has a large majority in these counties, yet Mr. Wilson's personal popularity was such as to carry him far ahead of his competitor in the race for Senatorial honors. Mr. Wilson is an old resident of California (about fifteen years, we believe); and in the county of Los Angeles, where he has lived during that period, he has filled many important offices. In 1852, he was appointed by Mr. Fillmore one of the Indian Commissioners for this State, and in connection with that office he did a vast deal to ameliorate the condition of the Indians. An honester, purer-minded man never received Legislative honors in California or any other State.

[San Francisco *Alta California*, September 12, 1855.]

＊

How many thousands of horses were stolen in the years '50 '51 '52 '53 from the Ranches of San Ysabel, Santa Margarita, Los Flores, El Tamuel, San Jasinto, Agua Caliente and numerous other ranches in San Diego County? Who that has lived in this county, for the past five years, does not recollect the magnificent droves of horses stolen from San Bernardino, San Jose, El Chino, El Rincon, Santa Ana, El Neguil, the Verdugos, Tajunga, San Fernando, Cahuenga and every other exposed Rancho in this county? We well recollect of hearing of the robberies committed on the San Buenaventura and Santa Clara Rivers, in the county of Santa Barbara, the actual capture and spoilation of the Mission of San Buenaventura by the Indians, while Santa Ynez, Santa Rosa, Lompoc, Los Alamos and other exposed Ranchos in the same county were actually stripped of all their horses. The same Indians who would enter this county through Walkers pass to rob, would add novelty to their depredations, by descending through the pass of Buenavista into the exposed county of San Luis Obispo, and would leave only the saddle horses that were tied at the doors of the Rancheros. We are confident we are under the mark, when we estimate the loss of the southern counties, for the five years previous to the establishment of the Tejon Reserve, arising from the depredations of the Indians upon horses alone at 300,000 dollars, and when we add the loss of horned cattle, the insecurity of person and property, and the abandonment of the frontier settlements, this estimate is insignificant in comparison to the material and almost fatal check to the prosperity of these counties.

In the fall of 1853 the Sebastian Reservation was established and in three months thereafter Indians robberies had ceased. Since that time we do not believe that the wild Indians tribes have robbed a single hoof of stock of any kind. The Mission of San Fernando whose owners suffered in the four years previous to the establishment of Reserve, a loss of between four or five thousand head of horses, now brands in security their yet numerous stock. The Ranchos of San Francisco and Capuntos, from which had been driven all their horses to pasture in the vicinity of this city, pastured last spring upwards of seven hundred horses, while San Cayetano, Tin and La Liebre, formerly with out a single horse or beef now have their thousand head upon their thousand hills. Now, safely through the Tejon into the Tulare Valley, and right in to Stockton, the peaceable cattle drover in security passes with his herds, where in '52, two cattle drovers alone lost near two thousand head by a whole sale robbery of the Indians, who also attacked and murdered in their houses, at the Four Creeks six or eight Americans.

[Los Angeles *Star*, October 20, 1855, quoted in R. G. Cleland, *The Cattle on a Thousand Hills*, 2d ed., 68-69.]

*

JOHN B. WELLER TO B. D. WILSON

Washington, D. C., January 17, 1856

I recd. a letter from you in relation to the Sebastian Reserve some weeks since which owing to severe illness has been neglected.

There is no disposition whatever on the part of the Com. Indian affairs to abandon that reserve. Although it has not been as prosperous as was desirable so far as Collecting the Indians is Concerned, yet it has given peace & security to our people in that region and it would certainly be very unwise to abandon it. Knowing as I do the importance of that reservation to the protection of the people of Los Angeles, San Bernardino & San Diego I can never Consent to its removal.

As I am still ill & write with difficulty you will excuse this short note.

[Wilson Papers, Huntington Library.]

*

JOHN M. BRIGHT TO ———

Kern River [n. d.]

I take this opportunity to inform you that we are all well at present, but not doing as well as we might. Times are squally here.—The Indians have broke out on the Four Creeks, and driven off a great many cattle. They have stolen three or four hundred head of horses from Santa Barbara, and carried them up into the mountains on Tule River. The miners on Kern River have quit work and forted up. There have been two fights on Four Creeks, and the Americans were whipped both times. An Express came in from Kern River this morning. They expect to be attacked in a day or two.

The settlers have all gathered into my house.—We hardly know what to do. I think you had better come up and get your cattle and take them to a more safe place. I am sure that all the stock in this valley will be stolen in a few days. Uncle Davy Smith is going to start for Los Angeles in the morning with a letter from the miners at Kern River to the Sheriff at Los Angeles, to raise a company to come to their assistance. If you come up, I want you to bring me five or six pounds of lead.

[Los Angeles *Star*, May 10, 1856, quoted in R. G. Cleland, *The Cattle on a Thousand Hills*, 2d ed., 69.]

*

Amount of grains &c., raised on Tejon Reserve, A. D. 1856, ending June 30

Wheat	475	acres
Barley	290	"
Potatoes	6	"
Corn	156	"
Vineyard	1	"
Peas	2	"
Beans	4½	"

Melons	2½ acres
Onions	½ "
Pea nuts	¼ "
Tomatoes	¼ "
Cabbages	½ "
General Garden	3 "
Fruit trees	600

[*Report of the Commissioner of Indian Affairs*, 1856, p. 249.]

*

CAVE J. COUTS TO THOMAS J. HENLEY

[*Guajomito*] *July* 7, 1856

The inhabited portion of this county [San Diego] is infested with two tribes of Indians known as the *San Luisenians*, and Dieguinos, according to the mission to which they respectively belonged, and number about 2,500 each. The San Luisenians exist in the northern part of the county, and, from the coast east, include the principal chain of mountains. These Indians are probably more advanced than any pertaining to your superintendency, and require but little attention with *proper management*. They understand the cultivation of the soil, and are the main dependence of our rancherios for vaqueros. They live comfortably in rancheros of tule (some few in adobes,) on what they gather from their wheat and barley fields, gardens, acorns and *cattle stealing*. Many of them can read and write. The Dieguinos, although reared in an adjoining mission, are far inferior to the San Luisenians. They lack nothing of that laziness and indolence proverbial to all Indian tribes, and live principally by cattle stealing, and on acorns. They are in the southern part of that county, and extend from the coast to the desert, where they naturally blend with the Yumas, with whom they are on very friendly terms.

[*Report of the Commissioner of Indian Affairs*, 1856, p. 240.]

*

JOHN RAINS TO THOMAS J. HENLEY

Temecula, July 24, 1856

Of the San Luis Rey Indians, there are in all belonging to this between twenty-five and twenty-eight hundred; they live in nineteen different rancherias, having a captain and alcalde in each, and one headman over all. They are Christians; raised to work; all cultivate more or less; all are good horsemen, and make good servants; very fond of liquor, easily managed when sober, but great fools when drinking. This year their crops have failed, owing to the want of water. There are some of them in a starving condition, and are obliged to steal to maintain themselves and families. The country of the San Luis Rey Indians, is joined by the country of the Cowela [Cahuilla] and Diegena Indians. They are about six thousand, all told.

[*Report of the Commissioner of Indian Affairs*, 1856, p. 243.]

*

THOMAS J. HENLEY TO
COMMISSIONER G. W. MANYPENNY

San Francisco, September 4, 1856

... In regard to the system of colonizing and subsisting Indians on reservations, I have only to say that it has so far succeeded entirely beyond my expectations, and is, in my judgment, the only system that can be of any real benefit to the Indians. It enables the government to withdraw them from the contaminating influences of an unrestrained intercourse with the whites, and gives an opportunity to provide for them just such, and no more, assistance than their wants from time to time may actually require....

[*Report of the Commissioner of Indian Affairs*, 1856, pp. 236-46.]

*

THE INDIANS OF SOUTHERN CALIFORNIA

For a couple of weeks back we have been publishing portions of a very interesting paper upon the condition of the Indians of Southern California. It is a report made out by Mr. Wilson, in the year 1852, addressed to Lieut. Beale, at that time Indian Agent for the State of California. The information contained in this document is not only interesting as it concerns the aboriginal races of Southern California, but it is highly important in a historical point of view, as showing the condition of the country in the early days treated of.

This report was transmitted at the time to the authorities at Washington, and was the foundation for the recommendations made by the Agent for the establishment of the Tejon Reservation, and the building of the military post at Fort Tejon. The reservation system was recommended by the author; but the military post was an afterthought, and as we take it, was as little contemplated by him, as it was useful or necessary to carry out the designes of the reservation plan.

We reprint the document for its intrinsic value, and not for any bearing it may have had on the system pursued by Government in its treatment of the Indians. It is well worth preserving, and will be found very useful to a full understanding of the early history of this portion of the State. It suggests a melancholy reflection upon the destiny of the red man, when one contemplates the scattered remnants of what were once numerous nations.

The report will be continued through several more numbers of the STAR.

[Editorial, Los Angeles *Star*, August 1, 1868.]

BIBLIOGRAPHY

BIOGRAPHICAL DATA on Benjamin Davis Wilson are contained in the collected correspondence of many of his contemporaries, but particularly in the Wilson Papers in the Huntington Library. For his early career the basic document is his "Observations on Early Days in California and New Mexico," a dictation for Hubert Howe Bancroft in 1877, MS, Bancroft Library, and available in Robert G. Cleland, *Pathfinders* (Los Angeles, 1929), 371-416, and, with annotations by Arthur Woodward, in Historical Society of Southern California, *Annual Publication for* 1934, pp. 74-150. A review and appraisal of his career may be found in John Walton Caughey, "Don Benito Wilson, an Average Southern Californian," *Huntington Library Quarterly*, II (1939), 285-300. See also Melbourne F. Aitken, "Benjamin D. Wilson, Southern California Pioneer" (M. A. thesis, U.C.L.A., 1948).

On southern California in the fifties the chief accumulations of information are in manuscript sources such as the Stearns Papers and the Wilson Papers in the Huntington Library, in the broken files of the early newspapers, and in Benjamin Hayes' Scrapbooks, now a part of the Bancroft Library. Horace Bell's *Reminiscences of a Ranger* (Los Angeles, 1881) and *On the Old West Coast* (New York, 1930) give a free-flowing, colored, and uninhibited account of early Los Angeles as he saw it. Harris Newmark's *Sixty Years in Southern California* (Boston, 1930), combining recollections with gleanings from the newspaper files, is more of a grab-bag, but an anecdotal introduction to the period. Two recent monographs are most useful. William B. Rice, *The Los Angeles Star*, 1851-1864 (Berkeley, 1947), charts the beginnings of journalism in Los Angeles and in the process accurately mirrors southern California life. Robert G. Cleland, *The Cattle on a Thousand Hills* (San Marino, 1941; rev. ed., 1951), is even more effective as a social history of southern California in the period of transition to American ways. For the San Bernardino district an important supplement is George William Beattie and Helen Pruitt Beattie, *Heritage of the Valley* (Pasadena, 1939).

Alfred L. Kroeber, *Handbook of the Indians of California* (Washington, 1925), contains authoritative information on almost all phases of southern California Indian culture. An older work of much interest because of the author's success in grasping the spirit of the Indians is Stephen

Powers, *The Indian Tribes* (Washington, 1877). David P. Barrows, *The Ethno-Botany of the Coahuilla Indians of Southern California* (Chicago, 1900), describes the Indians of the interior. Gerónimo Boscana, *Chinigchinich*, in various printings, of which the most convenient is the one annotated by Mark R. Harrington (Santa Ana, 1933), is a Franciscan's description of the Luiseño and Gabrielino. Hugo Reid's letters on the Indians of Los Angeles County, serialized in the Los Angeles *Star* in 1852, shortly before Wilson's report was written, were put into book form by Arthur Ellis (Los Angeles, 1926) and reproduced in Susanna Bryant Dakin, *Scotch Paisano* (Berkeley, 1939). Several studies by Sherburne F. Cook of the factors in population decline among the California Indians were published in *Ibero-Americana* (Berkeley, 1937-1943).

Zephyrin Engelhardt, *The Missions and Missionaries of California* (4 vols., San Francisco, 1908-1915), and the same author's volumes on individual missions have information on almost every phase of mission activities. More summary accounts are available in such works as Charles E. Chapman, *A History of California, The Spanish Period* (New York, 1921), and John Walton Caughey, *California* (New York, 1940). For analysis of the mission purpose see Herbert E. Bolton, "The Mission as a Frontier Institution in Spanish America," in his *Wider Horizons in American History* (New York, 1939).

The effects of American Indian policy as brought to bear in California are evaluated in Hubert Howe Bancroft, *History of California* (7 vols., San Francisco, 1884-1890), VII, 474-95, and in Caughey, *California*, 379-91. For a more detailed discussion see William H. Ellison, "The Federal Indian Policy in California, 1846-1860," *Mississippi Valley Historical Review*, IX (1922), 37-67; "The California Indian Frontier," *Grizzly Bear*, March 1922; and "Rejection of California Indian Treaties," *ibid.*, May-July, 1925. The California problem is discussed in relation to that of the West in general in Alban W. Hoopes, *Indian Affairs and Their Administration, with Special Reference to the Far West*, 1849-1860 (Philadelphia, 1932), and Edward Everett Dale, *The Indians of the Southwest* (Norman, 1949). For Edward F. Beale and the reservation experiment at Tejon see Helen S. Giffen and Arthur Woodward, *The Story of El Tejon* (Los Angeles, 1942), and Stephen Bonsal, *Edward Fitzgerald Beale: A Pioneer in the Path of Empire* (New York, 1912).